PREPPER'S
SURVIVAL HACKS

PREPPER'S
SURVIVAL HACKS

50 DIY Projects
for Lifesaving Gear, Gadgets and Kits

Jim Cobb

Ulysses Press

Published in the US by:
Ulysses Press
P.O. Box 3440
Berkeley, CA 94703
www.ulyssespress.com

ISBN: 978-1-61243-496-4
Library of Congress Control Number: 2015937561

Printed in the United States by Bang Printing

10 9 8 7 6 5 4 3 2 1

Acquisitions editor: Keith Riegert
Managing editor: Claire Chun
Editor: Renee Rutledge
Proofreader: Lauren Harrison
Design and layout: what!design @ whatweb.com
Cover artwork: from shutterstock.com; nuts and bolts © Viktor Gladkov, screw heads set © DeCe, cotton cable cord © Szasz-Fabian Ilka Erika, utility knife © Aleksandr Stepanov, hacksaw © humbak, plastic bottles © yalayama, newspapers © xamnesiacx, batteries © silabob
Index: Sayre Van Young

Distributed by Publishers Group West

For Tammy. Every day, I fall for you just a little bit more.

CONTENTS

INTRODUCTION

This book is very different from the others I've written. Many readers of my previous books have asked for more photos. The thing is, in my other books, there really wasn't a whole lot that warranted illustration. I mean, sure, I could have included some sort of stock photo of a bunch of people standing around to accompany the topic of group versus individual survival planning. But, really, would that photo have added any true value to the book?

As an author, I've always tried to be conscious of what I'm providing to the reader in exchange for their hard-earned dollars. As a reader myself, I've been suckered more than once by a flashy cover and some nifty graphics, only to find the text lacking. Too many writers look at photos and graphics as padding, rather than as actually adding value to the book. They look at photos, charts, diagrams, and all that fun stuff as a great way to add pages to the book, and that's about it. While a picture might indeed be worth a thousand words, it doesn't necessarily follow that a picture can fully replace all of those words. A great example of how photos are *supposed* to work can be found in any of my good friend John McCann's books, such as his excellent *Practical Self-Reliance*. He not only understands when a photo is needed, he's one hell of a photographer.

Leafing through the book you're holding (or scrolling through the pages on your tablet), you'll no doubt notice there are a ton of photos. To be honest, this book was a pain in the butt to create because of all those pictures. I'm not a photographer. I have a couple of friends who are, and they no doubt cringe and wince at any photos I post online or share with them. The composition is likely all messed up and the photo probably isn't framed the way it should be.

Here's the thing, though. The photos contained in this book aren't meant to hang on the wall of your kitchen or den. I hold no illusions that anyone could look at a photo here and think it in any way approaches *art*. To my way of thinking, as long as the photos allow you to follow the bouncing ball and complete the projects, they've served their purpose.

As for the projects themselves, there's some pretty neat stuff here. Some of it you may have seen before. I know the Milk Jug Lantern made the rounds online a while back. Why did I include it here? Two reasons, actually. First, there are going to be at least some readers of this book who've not seen it before. Second, part of the purpose of this book is to give you a resource to use during a disaster and the recovery period. Facebook and Google might not be viable options at that point. You might be in need of some sort of ambient lighting during an extended power outage and remember, "Hey, one of Cobb's books had a few lanterns in it!"

Other projects are likely to be brand-spankin' new to you. I've searched high and low for interesting ways to repurpose and recycle stuff you can find around the house and have put my own twists on a few ideas as well. Keep in mind, too, that the purpose of this book is *doing*, not just reading. Get up off your butt and actually try some of these projects. See what works for you and what doesn't. Few things in this book, if any, are truly universal. Every reader comes to the table with their own skill set, experience level, and individual circumstances.

Every project I chose to include in this book can be done by the average person. None require some sort of obscure tool or years of experience with carpentry, plumbing, or any other trade. In fact, just about any project in this book could be completed by a middle schooler. While some of the projects might be decidedly simplistic, they all work and will accomplish the intended goal. That's the whole point, right?

I'd love to hear from you and find out how you've fared with some of the projects in this book, as well as any you've come up with on your own. I answer all of my emails myself and maintain my own Facebook and Twitter accounts. If you send me a message, you can be assured it will reach me, not just some virtual assistant.

Email: Jim@survivalweekly.com

Facebook: Facebook.com/JimCobbSurvival

Twitter: Twitter.com/SurvivalWeekly

Web: SurvivalWeekly.com

One last thing. When you're working on these projects, please exercise common sense and good judgment. Make full use of the appropriate safety gear. Any time you're using tools, wear safety goggles. If you're cutting metal, whether with tin snips or a saw, make sure you're wearing gloves. While I want to hear about your successful projects, I really don't want you sending me pictures of lopped off fingers or the 72 stitches you needed after your failed attempt at making a Hobo Stove.

Have fun with this stuff, folks. Let your imagination run wild, get creative, and see what comes to mind after you've seen what others have done.

WATER

Common wisdom dictates that the human body can survive about three days without hydration. While that may be true in a technical sense, in the real world, the last day or two of that time period would be spent in agony and delirium. Don't ever try to ration water. If you have potable water available, drink it. The problem with rationing is that doing so may hinder your ability to search for more water sources. A far better plan is to keep your body running as efficiently as possible as you attempt to locate additional supplies.

It is almost as important to understand that water from natural sources, such as rivers, lakes, and ponds, absolutely must be treated before consumption. Failure to do so puts you at risk for some pretty serious health issues, such as giardia and cryptosporidium. The best way to treat water prior to drinking is to boil it. This will kill anything that might be in the water that could harm you. There is no need to let it boil for several minutes, either. Just bringing it to a rolling boil is sufficient.

Of course, there are several commercial products you could purchase that will filter and disinfect your water. These include various products sold by LifeStraw, Berkey, and Sawyer. All work very well and are worthy of purchase. The trick is to make sure you have the filter device with you any time you venture into the field, just in case. That snazzy new water filtration straw does utterly no good sitting on a shelf at home while you're dying of thirst sitting next to a pond.

Another important consideration is to carry some sort of container you can use to transport water. Many of us routinely carry some sort of water bottle with us when hiking, so that poses little issue. However, I strongly advise you to consider investing in a stainless steel water bottle rather than relying on something made from plastic. While it is possible to boil water in a plastic container if you know what you're doing and you're careful, it is far easier and safer to do so using a steel bottle.

A product I wholeheartedly endorse is the Aqua-Pouch, designed, produced, and sold by Survival Resources. It is basically a heavy-duty plastic bag that folds up small and flat. Keep it in your kit and you'll always have a container you can use to transport water. It holds up to 1 liter, which coincidentally is the same measurement many water treatment products utilize.

Water is a necessity for life. It is important to plan ahead so you have the means to collect and disinfect it. The first two projects in this section will focus on water collection, followed by two projects on DIY filtration devices.

« TRANSPIRATION BAG »

While you're not going to get a ton of water with a single transpiration bag, you can get a fair amount of bang for your buck by putting out several of them. Transpiration bags use the sun's heat and energy to condense moisture from the plant and collect in the bag. They work all by themselves once they're set up. What seems to work well is to set them up in the morning and collect the water in the evening.

» MATERIALS

Clear garbage bag
Small stone

Twist ties or rope

#1 The first step is figuring out where you will put your transpiration bag(s). The ideal location would have a few deciduous trees in the immediate area—large ones with branches hanging down to where you can easily reach them.
Deciduous trees are the ones with leaves, as opposed to conifers, which have needles. Shrubs and bushes will also work, but the larger they are, the better. Also, take a few minutes to make sure the trees or shrubs aren't poisonous to you.

#2 Place the garbage bag over a few of the leaf-bearing branches, stuffing in as many as possible. Toss in a small stone and use it to pull one corner of the bag down toward the ground a bit. Secure the open end of the bag tightly against the branches using the twist ties or rope. You want this closure to be as airtight as possible.

#3 As the day goes on, the sun's rays will heat up the inside of the bag, forcing water from the leaves to condense on the sides of the bag. From there, it will trickle down to the rock-weighted corner. Depending upon conditions, you could see as little as 1 cup of water to as much as 1 quart or so.

#4 To get the water out of the bag, you can either remove the bag completely and carefully pour it out or snip a small hole in the corner, then tie the bag tightly above that cut after emptying the water.

#5 I don't like to keep a bag on the same tree for more than 1 or 2 days, provided I have other options for placing the bag. It puts stress on the tree, of course, and while my life is worth more to me than the life of that tree, if I don't have to put undue stress on it, I won't.

« SOLAR STILL »

I'm going to be flat-out honest with you. I don't in any way, shape, or form endorse the use of a solar still for acquiring water in a survival situation. I'm including it here for two reasons.

1 In any survival manual, it is almost expected that the solar still be mentioned, and its absence in this book would be noticeable.

2 I wanted to include it specifically so I could talk a bit about why you shouldn't rely upon it.

» MATERIALS

Shovel

Bucket or clean container

Large plastic tarp

Large rocks or logs

Small rock

#1 On the surface, the solar still is a fairly straightforward project. Using your shovel, dig a hole a few feet deep. At the bottom of the hole, roughly in the center, place your bucket or other clean container. Next, stretch the plastic tarp across the top of the hole using the large rocks or logs to secure it in place. Finally, place a small rock at the center of the tarp, which weighs it down above your container.

#2 The idea is that the sun will heat up the inside of that hole, causing moisture from the ground to evaporate, then condense on the bottom of the plastic tarp. It will then run along the plastic to the point above the bucket, into which it will drip.

Here's the thing. The amount of water you'll gain through the use of the solar still is, quite literally, a drop in the bucket compared to the amount of energy you'll expend by digging the hole and setting everything up.

Don't believe me? Go ahead, set one up tomorrow and see how well it performs. If you get more than 2 cups of water, you'll be doing fairly well.

« OSMOSIS WATER FILTER »

This isn't the greatest solution for water filtration, as it won't do anything about bacteria and such. However, it works fairly well at taking turbid, cloudy water, such as from a mud puddle, and turning it clear by removing sediment and debris. Plus, it works all by itself once you get it set up.

» MATERIALS

2 containers, such as pitchers, buckets, or glasses

Cotton rope, cotton bandanna, or paper towel

#1 Place the two containers side by side. Pour the dirty water into one container. Put one end of the cotton rope into the water and run the rope to the other container. The free end of the rope should dangle into the second container but not rest on the bottom.

#2 If you don't have cotton rope, a cotton bandanna or even a paper towel will do. To make things easier, I roll the bandanna up into a rope and use a few rubber bands spaced along the length to keep it in place. Here, I've done the quick and dirty version by rolling up a paper towel.

#3 It takes a while but water will gradually be soaked up into the rope or bandanna and make its way to the other end, dripping into the other container. The sediment and such will be left behind.

#4 I cannot stress enough, though, that the filtered water will still need to be purified in some way. Boiling is best, as that will kill pretty much anything in the water that could hurt you. All this filtration system does is remove the larger impurities, allowing your purification method to work that much more efficiently.

« LAYERED FILTER »

This project results in a quick and easy way to filter sediment and such out of water you've obtained from a pond, stream, or even a mud puddle. It does not, however, disinfect the water. You'll still need to boil it or use some other means to kill any parasites and other nasty stuff. Even though the parasites may be so small you can't see them, they will still ruin your day.

» MATERIALS

2-liter bottle

Razor knife

Hole puncher (optional)

Cotton bandanna or 1 to 2 coffee filters

Old sock or rag

Rock or rubber mallet

2 handfuls each of charcoal, sand, and gravel

#1 The 2-liter bottle should be empty and clean. It doesn't matter if the plastic is clear or green. Using the razor knife, cut off the bottom of the bottle. Once the filter is complete, it will be rather heavy, so you might also wish to punch  two holes near the now-open bottom so you'll be able to hang the filter using cord or wire. As you'll see in the following photos, I've balanced my filter on top of a small glass jar.

#2 Take the cotton bandanna and stuff it down inside the bottle, pushing it into the neck a bit. Alternatively, you could use one or two coffee filters in place of the bandanna.

#3 The next layer is charcoal. You can use any burnt wood from your wood stove, fireplace, or campfire, as long as that wood wasn't pressure treated, such as lumber used for outdoor projects. Do not use charcoal briquettes, either, as  they likely have been treated with chemicals to make them easy to light. Rather, just grab a few large chunks of charcoal from your campfire, place them in an old sock or rag, then smash them into small pieces with a rock or rubber mallet. You want your charcoal layer to be about 2 inches thick, and by breaking the chunks into smaller pieces, you prevent gaps where water could pour through without running through the charcoal.

#4 Next comes the sand layer. You can use regular sandbox sand for this, but the smaller the grains of sand, the better. So, if you have an opportunity to use something finer or softer than sandbox sand, go for it. As with the charcoal, this layer should be about 2 inches thick.

#5 Finally, add a layer of gravel. This layer should also be roughly 2 inches thick. Nothing fancy is needed, no special kind of gravel, but smaller stones are better than larger ones. Just collect a couple of handfuls from the ground, rinse them off, and toss them into the bottle.

#6 Some people like to repeat the sand and gravel layers. I've even seen a layered filter where a coffee filter was used between each of the layers. Honestly, all of that's probably overkill, but if you have the resources available and are so inclined, have at it.

#7 To use, hang the filter above a clean container. Slowly pour water into the filter and let gravity do the rest. You'll probably notice that this isn't a fast filtration process. It is best to pour some water in, then go off and do something else for a bit.

#8 Again, the filtered water still needs to be boiled or treated in some way before consumption. Filtering the water in this way helps to lengthen the life of your purchased water disinfection gear, as that equipment won't need to work quite as hard to make the water potable.

FOOD ACQUISITION

In this section, I'm going to talk about a few different projects that will help you grow or otherwise obtain food. Most of these projects aren't suited for last-minute solutions when you're starving, but instead are things you can implement today so you're ahead of the game later. I firmly believe you can grow at least *some* amount of food, no matter where you live. It is just a matter of trying different approaches until you find one that works for you. Many urban dwellers have very successful patio gardens, using various containers to house their veggies and fruits.

For the meat-eaters, we have a couple of projects for fish and game acquisition. Please note, there are laws on the books that govern when you can and cannot harvest wild critters. While these laws might be rather low priority in the aftermath of a major disaster, they are still laws and there are potential penalties for breaking them. Use common sense and remember any legal issues that arise are yours and yours alone to sort out.

I'm also going to talk about food you can store for later use, such as DIY Meals Ready to Eat (MREs) for your bug out bag. Using a DIY approach ensures you'll not only save money, but that you'll actually want to eat what you have packed away.

Our bodies use calories as fuel. While many of us have an excess of fuel around our middles and thus are in little danger of starving to death in just a couple of days, tummy rumbles tend to be a distraction. We need to be able to focus on more important matters in the aftermath of a disaster. Planning ahead for food needs is a great help in that regard.

« POCKET FISHING KIT »

You'd have to search long and hard to find a fishing kit that is smaller than this one. When you're done, you'll have a tiny container holding sinkers, hooks, line, and even a couple of small, artificial lures if that strikes your fancy.

» MATERIALS

Razor knife or hacksaw

2 plastic soda bottles with caps, any size

Fine-grit sandpaper

Hot glue gun or epoxy

Old gift card or credit card

Marker

Scissors

Braided fishing line

Split shot sinkers

Hooks and/or lures

#1 Start by cutting the tops off of each of the soda bottles. A hacksaw works best, though you might be able to make do with a razor knife. Cut just behind the plastic lip or ridge and try to make the cut as straight as possible.

#2 Next, sand down the cut sides of the bottle tops. They don't need to be perfect, but the smoother, the better.

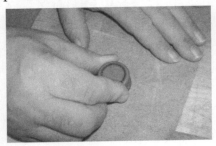 

#3 Once that's done, plug in the glue gun to heat up. Then, place the cut side of one of the bottle tops on the gift card. Use the marker to draw a circle around the bottle top and cut out the circle with the scissors.

#4 Run a bead of glue or epoxy around the perimeter of the circle you cut from the gift card, then place one of the bottle tops over it, gluing it in place. Once the glue has dried, flip the top over and do the same to the other side.

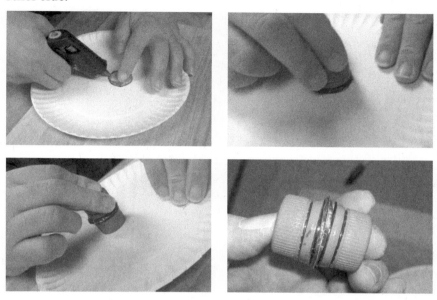

#5 Now, you *could* stop right here. What you have at this point is a nifty little storage container, suitable for things like tinder or meds. You could even omit the plastic disk and have a larger, single interior rather than one that is double-sided. But, I promised you a fishing kit, so here's how to finish it up.

#6 On the bottle tops, you'll see a plastic ring that sits just under the cap. Cut that ring off one of the tops. Then, tie on some fishing line and wind it around the bottle top, right at the spot where the ring was removed. Be careful to keep the line from winding on the threads as that may prevent the cap from twisting on securely. When I made this one, I stopped at 55 feet of line. Crimp a split shot sinker on the loose end of the line and drop it into the bottle top, then screw down the cap. This keeps the line from unraveling. I recommend using braided fishing line for this project. Monofilament line has a problem with "memory" and will tend to kink up if stored in this fashion for a time.

#7 Unscrew the other cap and inside you can store your hooks, sinkers, and lures. Granted, there's not a ton of empty space to use for storage, but you might be surprised at just how much you can carry in this tiny kit.

« DIY MRE »

Originally designed for the military, MREs have become quite popular with the prepper crowd, though I'm not entirely sure why that is. They taste... okay. But they are expensive and actually fairly heavy to carry around in your pack. Some folks open them up and remove the main courses, just carrying those. That's not a bad plan. If you decide to go with commercially produced MREs, though, I highly suggest you take the time to try them out and make sure you like the taste, as well as ensure they agree with your digestive system.

In this project, we're going to put together our own version of MREs, using the foods we already know we like and that we know aren't going to give us...issues...later.

» MATERIALS

Shelf-stable foods

Large (quart- or gallon-size) zip-top plastic bags

Plastic cutlery

Paper towels or napkins

#1 The types of food you include in your MRE depend on what you like to eat and whether you want to include foods that will require some type of cooking prior to consumption. Examples of common DIY MRE components include:

Bouillon cubes

Candy

Canned meat (e.g., Spam)

Crackers

Dried fruits

Dried nuts

Instant oatmeal

Instant single-serve drink mixes

Packaged instant potatoes

Packaged noodles

Pouched meat (e.g., tuna, chicken)

Single-serve salt and pepper

Ramen noodles

Vitamins

Tea bags

#2 Stick with things that require nothing more than water for preparation. You aren't likely to have butter, milk, and other niceties with you during a bug out. Things like salt and pepper can be either saved from fast food meals or packaged yourself using a variation of the Fire Straws instructions found on page 63.

#3 Group your selections into different meals, striving for at least a little diversity so you're not eating the same thing each time. Another important consideration is meal preparation and what you plan to have available to you for  that purpose. If you're only going to have a single small cooking pot in your pack, don't plan on making two different things that require the use of that pot for a single meal.

#4 Once you have the items sorted into individual meals, package them up using one large zip-top bag for each meal. For some items, such as plastic forks and spoons, vitamins, and bouillon cubes, you may want to use small, snack-size  zip-top bags within the larger bag to keep things organized.

#5 Some folks like to use vacuum sealers to preserve their DIY MREs. That's certainly an excellent option if you have a sealer and bags available to you. However, using the large zip-top bags and gently squeezing the air out of them prior  to sealing them shut should suffice. Most of the components of your MRE are already in their own sealed packaging.

« BOLA »

I have no doubt you've seen bolas used on TV or in the movies. A traditional tool of Argentinian cowboys (gauchos), bolas are used to ensnare cattle or game. While they differ in size, bolas all consist of a number of weights connected by cordage. They are typically thrown at the legs of the targeted animal. The weights wrap around and trip up the animal.

In various cultures, bolas have been used for hunting and even as battle weapons. The traditional bola is made using wooden balls or leather sacks of rocks for the weights. We're going to make it a lot easier on ourselves and just use stuff we have in our garage.

The most common version of the bola uses three weighted ends, so that's what we're going to do in this project. However, once you understand the basic mechanics of the bola, feel free to make others using additional weights.

» MATERIALS

2 pieces (4-feet and 2-feet) thin rope

Handful or two of nuts and washers

#1 Start with the longer piece of rope and tie a knot about 6 inches from one end.

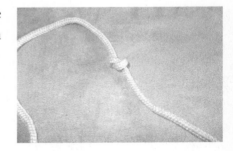

#2 Thread a few nuts and washers onto the rope, then tie another knot on the loose end, jamming the nuts and washers tightly between the knots. Repeat this with the opposite end of the rope.

#3 Take the 2-foot piece of rope and repeat the above step on one end. Reduce the nuts and washers that you use here a bit. Traditionally, the weight on this part of the bola should be less than the weight on the other ends.

#4 Find the midpoint of the 4-foot piece of rope. Tie the short piece to the long piece at that point. I've found that it works well to use a knot to tie off the short piece, then do a quick overhand knot with the long piece over that. Doing so will prevent the short piece from sliding up and down the long piece.

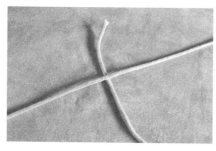 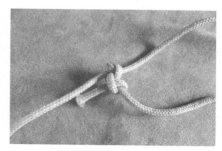

#5 To use the bola, grasp the middle length of cordage by the weighted end, twirl the bola over your head a few times, and then release it in a throwing motion in the direction of the target. Make no mistake, it takes practice to be able to hit a stationary, much less moving, target.

« COLD FRAME »

A cold frame is basically a type of greenhouse. In fact, traditionally they were built alongside a greenhouse and used to harden off seedlings that had been started in the larger structure. Today, many people use cold frames to extend the growing season, particularly in the colder northern climes.

This is one project where I truly can't give you exact, step-by-step instructions because the cold frame is largely dependent upon the materials available. Many people use an old window obtained from either their own or another homeowner's remodeling project. Alternatively, you could fashion together a window using clear plastic like Lexan.

» MATERIALS

Window
Lumber
Weather-resistant screws
Insulation, such as small bales of straw
　(optional)

#1 The basic idea here is to build a box with a clear lid, ideally angled toward the sun. In the United States, this means the lid would face the south. The lid allows the sun's energy to heat up the inside of the box, and angling the lid

helps gather more of that energy. Plus, an angled lid lets rain slide off.

#2 Some people go so far as to add some insulation to the outside of the box, such as small bales of straw. It is important, though, to make sure you open the lid when the weather is nice to allow for air flow.

#3 Most cold frames are built so the lid is hinged, making it easy to open and close. This isn't a necessity, though, and you could simply build a box and rest the window on top of it.

#4 It stands to reason that your cold frame box can be no larger than the available window or other clear lid you have. The box itself should be built using weather-resistant wood, such as cedar, if possible. Most cold frames don't have a bottom on them and are just built directly on the ground. That being the case, it is important to protect the wood from moisture if it isn't naturally resistant. I don't like using treated lumber for projects that will contain things I may be eating at some point. If you don't have or cannot afford cedar, you can paint the wood to protect it from the elements.

#5 Use weatherproof screws; otherwise, you may find your cold frame is falling apart within a year or less.

#6 As for height of the box, 1 or 2 feet should be sufficient. Any higher and you're wasting energy by just heating air instead of plants and soil.

« SEED TAPE »

Seed tape is a great tool for increasing the efficiency of your gardening efforts. You can buy seed tape, of course. But you can produce the same thing for far cheaper if you're willing to put in just a bit of time and effort. There are two distinct advantages to using seed tape in the garden. First, it largely eliminates the need for thinning as seedlings come up. Second, many seeds, such as lettuce and carrots, are extremely small. So small, in fact, that you almost can't help over-seeding the area. Seed tape allows you to conserve your supply, which could be vitally important in any sort of extreme, long-term crisis.

» MATERIALS

1 packet of seeds
Toilet paper
Ruler
Marker
Flour
Water
Toothpick or small twig
Tweezers

#1 Look at the back of your seed packet or consult another source to find out how far apart your seeds are supposed to be planted. Roll out a few feet of toilet paper on a table and fold it in half lengthwise. You'll be placing your seeds on half of that strip.

#2 Use the ruler and marker to make a dot where each seed will be placed. Here, we're using carrot seeds, which should be planted 1 inch apart.

#3 Next, you'll make your glue using the flour and water. Mix them at a ratio of two parts flour, one part water. You won't need much, maybe 2 tablespoons of flour and 1 of water.

#4 Use a toothpick or small twig to place a small dot of glue on the marks you made on the toilet paper. Then, use the tweezers to pick up and drop a single seed onto each spot of glue.

#5 Alternatively, you could dip the toothpick in the glue, use it to pick up a seed, then wipe the glue and seed on the toilet paper.

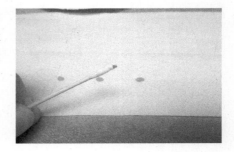

#6 When you get to the end of the toilet paper, place a few drops of glue at both ends of the paper, then fold it over to seal the seeds inside. Let this sit out for a few hours or overnight so the glue can dry completely.

 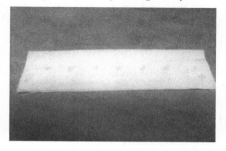

#7 To use, dig a small trench in your garden to the prescribed depth, lay down the seed tape, and cover it with soil. Tamp down the soil a bit to make sure everything stays in place. Water regularly and soon you'll have seedlings breaking through, all properly spaced without any thinning required.

« GROWING FOOD FROM »
KITCHEN SCRAPS

As a general rule of thumb, we as a society throw away a lot of stuff, don't we? Now granted, many of us make diligent use of compost bins so a fair amount of the organic "trash" is reused. But, did you know you can sort of skip a step and grow food directly from some of your kitchen scraps?

There are literally dozens of fruits and vegetables that can be grown from scraps. I'm only going to talk about a handful of them here. If this is something that interests you, get online and do some research to find more things you can grow.

Please note, it is always best to seek out and purchase heirloom varieties of fruits and vegetables whenever possible. Many of the fruits and veggies sold today are actually hybrids. Because of this, the seeds and such won't necessarily grow true. In fact, they might not grow at all. Think of heirloom varieties as being pure-blooded and hybrids as mutts. In this case, unlike with dogs, mutts are bad.

ROMAINE LETTUCE

Cut or tear the stalks so as to leave a stump about 2 inches high from the bottom. Poke three toothpicks into the bottom of the stump or stalk to make sort of a tripod shape. Place the stalk into a bowl or glass and fill with water to about halfway up the stalk. The stalk should be resting on the toothpicks. Put the bowl or glass on a windowsill or some other location that gets plenty of sunshine. Within just a few days, you'll see new growth starting at the top. Dump out the water and add fresh every day. Once the roots begin to develop, remove the toothpicks and transfer the plant to either a pot or right into the garden.

CELERY

This one is almost identical to growing romaine lettuce. Cut the celery so as to leave a stump 2 inches to 3 inches high. Place this in a shallow dish with the cut side facing up. Fill the dish with water about halfway up the stalk. Celery grows fairly quick in the beginning. Leave the dish in a sunny spot and you'll notice new growth from the center of the stalk within a couple of days. Once the new growth is about an inch high or so, transfer the stump to soil. Water it regularly and you'll have harvestable celery within a few months.

POTATOES

Most of us already know this, but you can grow a mess of taters from just one, if you know what you're doing. Simply cut up the potato into chunks, with at least one eye per chunk. Let these sit out for a few days to dry out, then plant in soil with the eyes facing up. Potatoes are slow growers, so be patient.

GARLIC

When you buy garlic, you will get several cloves. Take one of them and plant it in soil with the roots (the flat part of the clove) facing down and the pointy end facing up. Cover with about an inch of soil. Keep the container of soil in an area with direct sunlight and water it regularly. You'll soon see green growth coming up. Clip this growth when it gets to about 3 inches high, leaving about an inch to regrow. Eventually, this will stop growing and dry up. That's when you'll know the cloves are ready to be harvested. Each clove you plant will result in an entire bulb (several cloves) of garlic.

ONIONS

Slice off the root end of the onion, leaving about ½ inch or so of onion attached to it. Plant this in soil with the roots facing down. It shouldn't be planted very deep, just an inch or so beneath the surface. It will take about three months to grow and mature into a new onion. When the aboveground growth turns yellow, that's when you'll know it is time to harvest.

GREEN ONIONS

After you've chopped off the green part of the onion, put the remaining white bulb in water with the root end facing down. A narrow drinking glass works great for this. Find one at a thrift store if you don't have one at home. Keep the glass in a sunny spot and change the water every couple of days. Soon, you'll see roots forming at the base and green growth starting at the top.

GINGER

This one is about a simple as it gets. Few people use an entire ginger root before it begins to go bad. Just cut off what you need, then plant the remaining root in soil with the buds facing up. Unless you live in a very warm, humid environment, this will be an indoor plant for you. As it grows, the roots will spread out. It will take about four months of growth before you'll be harvesting new ginger. When that time comes, just cut off what you need and cover the rest with soil again.

« TAKE-OUT CONTAINER »
GREENHOUSE

Many of us purchase take-out food at least once or twice a month, perhaps even weekly. Often, these plastic containers are just about perfect for making little greenhouses for seed starting or growing herbs. Repurposing the containers in this way helps to reduce what ends up in landfills, too.

Without getting into the science at work, suffice it to say that greenhouses work by turning the sun's energy into heat and trapping it, warming the soil and plants inside the structure. The take-out container you use for this project must have a transparent lid so as to allow the sun's rays through. In fact, depending upon your situation, you might only need to use the lid.

» MATERIALS
Take-out container
Seeds
Soil

#1 Wash the container and lid thoroughly to remove any and all food residue. I like to use newspaper pots (see sidebar) for seed starting. If the container is deep enough with the lid on, you can simply place your newspaper pot in the container and cover it with the lid. Remove the lid as needed for watering. You should also allow for adequate airflow by either propping up one end of the lid or poking a few holes.

« NEWSPAPER POTS »

Newspaper can be recycled and made into small pots that are perfect for seed starting. The easiest method involves using The Pot Maker, which is a handy little device you can find almost anywhere garden tools are sold, including online. Simply use Google to find one near you. The way it works is rather simple. A strip of newspaper is wrapped around a wide dowel, with the bottom edge of the strip overhanging about two inches on the bottom of the dowel. The overhanging paper is then folded over and crimped, making a flat bottom. The newspaper pot is slid from the dowel and placed into a container, then filled with soil and a seed.

Once the seedling is sufficiently mature to be transferred outside, the whole newspaper pot is placed into the ground. It will decompose as the plant grows.

#2 Another option is to simply fill the container with soil and plant your seeds. Put the container on a windowsill where it will get sunshine daily and you're all set. Obviously, make sure to keep the container covered to warm the soil and plants. Don't forget to water the seeds, either.

#3 You can also use these outside in the garden. We've placed them over seedlings we transplanted, as the lids will keep the plant warmer during the cold evenings in early spring.

COOKING

One of the first things to go in the aftermath of most disasters is ready access to things like electricity. With the power gone, your microwave oven, toaster oven, and even perhaps your stovetop are all useless. If you have a charcoal or gas grill, you're still in business. Grills can be used to cook more than just steaks and ribs—you do know that, right?

In addition to grills, so many people have patio fire pits you'd think it was mandated by law. These work great as portable campfires. With the right gear, you can cook darn near anything on them.

But what if the grill and the patio fire pit were both buried under 2 feet of snow? What if the temperatures outside were south of zero and still falling? Or it had been raining for so long you expected animals to start filing, two by two, into the neighborhood?

The projects in this section might not allow you to put together a five-course meal on the fly, but they'll all boil water and heat a pot of soup. A couple of them, such as the Buddy Burner and the Altoids Tin Alcohol Stove, can be used indoors, provided you're in an average-size room with good ventilation. Others, like the Brick Rocket Stove and the Hobo Stove, need to be used outdoors due to the large flames and high heat generated.

Remember, though, that any time you're dealing with an open flame, due caution is advised. It's not the best time to engage in a round of tackle football with your kids, for example.

Also worth noting is the fact that most of your standard cookware isn't made for long-term use on an open flame. It might warp a bit and it will almost surely become soot-covered on the bottom. You can help with the latter by rubbing a bar of soap on the bottom of the pan prior to use. If you were cooking over an actual campfire or even your patio fire pit, the goal would be to cook over hot coals rather than flames. With these projects, though, you don't really have that option. You'll be using fire, not coals, to heat your pan and your food.

If you have the opportunity to purchase one or two pieces of cast-iron cookware, I highly encourage you to do so. First, they are very well-suited for cooking over an open flame. Second, everything just tastes better cooked in cast iron. Try it and I'm sure you'll agree.

« BUDDY BURNER »

This project results in a handy little cooking implement that is great for when the power goes out and the weather prohibits using the patio grill or even a campfire. Plus, this is a fun project for the kids in the family.

» MATERIALS

Corrugated cardboard
Knife or scissors
Empty tuna can
Old candles or crayons
Matches
Bricks or small rocks
Small pot lid or aluminum foil

#1 Start by cutting the corrugated cardboard into strips. The width of each strip should be about the same size as the depth of the inside of the tuna can. Corrugated cardboard is the type that consists of two thin sheets with what looks like ripples between them. When you cut the strips, you want to have those ripples visible along the long edges of the strips. In other words, when you look down along the long edge of the strip, you should see what looks like little holes all along the edge.

#2 As you're working on that, start melting your candles or crayons (see page 76).

#3 While the wax is melting, begin placing the cardboard strips into the tuna can. Start at the inside edge of the can and work your way toward the middle, wrapping the strips around and around. You want to end up with the entire  interior of the can filled with cardboard.

#4 Once the wax is completely melted, carefully pour it over the cardboard, filling each of those little holes. Then let the wax cool and harden.

#5 When it comes time to use the Buddy Burner, strike a match and hold it just above the wax, until you see the wax begin to melt a bit. Then, just lay the lit match in that spot and the wax will begin to burn. It might take a minute or  two but soon you'll have a fairly substantial flame.

#6 You don't want to put your cooking pot directly onto the Buddy Burner, as you'll smother the flame. Instead, use a couple of bricks or small rocks stacked on either side of the can to support the pot above the burner.

#7 The Buddy Burner is safe to use indoors, as all it amounts to is a giant candle. Of course, the normal warnings apply as to any sort of open flame indoors. Don't use this near curtains or other flammable objects.

#8 To extinguish the flame, simply cover it with a pot lid or even a piece of foil to smother the flame. The Buddy Burner will last quite a while without the need to refill it with more wax.

« BRICK ROCKET STOVE »

The next time you visit a garden center, pick up a small load of patio paver bricks. You'll need 20 of them for this project, which should run you all of about $10 or so. Color of the bricks doesn't matter, just get whatever appeals to you. You can keep them stacked in the corner of your garage until you need to assemble this quick-and-dirty rocket stove.

Rocket stoves come in many different shapes and sizes. At the core, though, they all share the same basic design. At the bottom, you'll have the burn chamber, into which fuel and air are fed. Rising up from the burn chamber is a chimney, which draw the heat from the flame upward, concentrating it on your cooking pot, which rests at the top of the chimney. A rocket stove is a very efficient tool for cooking off-grid, using a minimal amount of fuel for maximum results.

» MATERIALS

20 brick patio pavers
Wide masonry chisel
Hammer
Eye protection

Work gloves
Small sticks and twigs
Cotton balls or newspaper
Matches

#1 The first step in this project is also the most difficult—cutting one brick paver in half. When you buy the bricks, you could certainly ask if they could cut one for you. Some places might have such a service. But this fairly straightforward process takes just a minute or two to do at home. You will absolutely want to wear eye protection and work gloves when you break the brick. Small pieces of it will go flying.

#2 Start by measuring the halfway point on the brick, either by using a ruler or just eyeballing it, and drawing a cutting line using a piece of chalk or just scratching it out with a rock. This isn't open-heart surgery; don't worry about making things absolutely perfect. Using the chisel, score this line a few times. All that means is to use the chisel to make a groove along that cutting line. Hold the chisel in place along the line and lightly tap it several times with the hammer. It should begin to cut into the brick a bit after several taps. Some folks advocate doing the same thing on the opposite side of the brick, or even all four sides. Personally, I've not had a problem with just scoring one side and moving on from there.

#3 Once you have the cutting line scored to your satisfaction, line up the edge of your chisel in the groove. Making sure the chisel is as perpendicular to the brick as possible, give it one solid whack with the hammer. If all goes as planned, the brick will break into two pieces, right along the scored line. It won't be perfect, but that's okay, it doesn't need to be.

#4 Find a reasonably level spot for the rocket stove. It can be built right on the ground, but I advise you not to place it on grass or other flammable material. While the flame will be fully contained within the stove, small burning sticks may occasionally fall out and end up on the ground.

#5 This rocket stove is built in layers. All you're doing is dry stacking the bricks in a certain pattern for each layer. The first layer is the base, of course, and looks like this.

#6 Notice that you're using one of the half-bricks in the bottom layer. It really doesn't matter if the cut edge faces in or out.

#7 The next layer uses the other half-brick, like so.

#8 Then, the next two layers.

#9 Then, place two bricks on each side of the chimney opening at the top. This is where you'll place your cooking pot.

#10 Place one more brick at the bottom, in front of the fuel chamber opening. This gives you a shelf where you can position fuel.

#11 Your rocket stove is going to use small sticks and twigs for fuel. I like to use cotton balls or newspaper to help get the fire started. Toss some of that into the fuel chamber, then feed in a few thin sticks. Drop a lit match onto the cotton or newspaper to light the fire. As the fire burns, gradually add more sticks until the fire is hot and burning well.

#12 Place your cooking pot on top and away you go. Feed fuel into the chamber as needed. You'll want to pay close attention to that, in order to ensure a steady cooking fire. You can add a little more fuel or taper it down a bit as needed.

#13 You won't be able to cook several meals with this stove without cleaning it out from time to time. As you'll notice, the burn chamber isn't all that large and it will fill up with ash and charred fuel after a while. A true rocket stove is well-insulated and, as a result, there is usually very little ash and such left over. Our makeshift one here isn't quite that efficient. But it also costs just a few dollars and takes 5 minutes to assemble.

« HOBO STOVE »

The hardest part of this project might be finding a metal coffee can. They seem to be getting increasingly rare as more and more companies are converting to plastic containers. Other metal cans are suitable, such as #10 food cans or new, unused paint cans. I recommend you not use paint cans that have ever actually held paint or stain as the fumes given off when the stove is burning may be toxic. You can find brand new paint cans at many hardware stores.

The Hobo Stove has been around for 100 years or so. It works very well for boiling water or heating a quick meal, using a minimal amount of fuel to do so.

» MATERIALS

Metal can
Drill and drill bits
Can opener
Tin snips
Wire hanger (optional, see instructions)
Safety goggles
Work gloves

#1 It should go without saying, but your metal can should be empty and clean. It doesn't need to be spotless, but it should be washed out reasonably well. With your safety goggles and work gloves on, start by drilling some air holes in the can. This doesn't require Pythagorean precision, but the holes should be roughly equidistant from each other. Make two rows of holes, one about 2 inches from the bottom and another about 2 inches from the top. You only need about six holes in each row.

#2 Next, remove the bottom of the can with the can opener. Do this after you've drilled the holes, as the bottom will provide some stability when you're drilling.

#3 Use the tin snips to cut out a section of the can at the bottom. This is where you'll be adding fuel once the stove is in use. Make it roughly 4 inches across and 2 inches high. Some folks like to cut this as a door, leaving it connected  along one side so it can be bent open or closed. I don't like doing that, as the metal is fairly sharp and I wouldn't want anyone to cut their hand as they're adding fuel to the fire. You can always use a rock or something to close off part of that opening if you want to slow the fire down a bit.

#4 You can see here where I crimped over the jagged edge left from the long cut. This is done by cutting approximately ¼ inch deeper on each side of the door. Start at one end of this thin flap and bend the metal over to the inside of the can.

#5 The Hobo Stove uses biomass for fuel. Biomass is just a fancy term for natural materials like twigs and bark. To use the stove, simply pile a bit of fuel at the bottom and light it up. Once the fire is burning, you'll add fuel through the open space on the side of the stove as needed. Your pot can rest right on top of the can as the holes you drilled should provide plenty of air flow for the fire.

#6 One modification I've seen some people do is to use a metal hanger to provide for a place to rest your cook pot. Simply cut two pieces of wire hanger long enough to stretch across the stove, with a little extra on each side. Drill four small holes, two on each side, each 1 inch from the top of the stove and about 3 inches apart. For these holes, you may indeed want to measure for the placement to ensure the holes are level. Feed the wire pieces through the holes and you'll have created something like a shelf upon which you can rest your cook pot.

« ALTOIDS TIN »
ALCOHOL STOVE

Alcohol stoves are great for off-grid food prep because just a little fuel goes a long way. Plus, there is little to no smoke from the flame. I've carried this stove, along with a plastic bottle of fuel, in my own bug out bag for a couple of years now. Just be sure the bottle you use for the fuel storage seals tightly. I recommend placing the sealed bottle inside a zip-top plastic bag, just in case it leaks.

» MATERIALS

Empty and clean Altoids tin

Perlite or vermiculite*

Window screen**

Marker

Scissors

Denatured alcohol

Matches

Small bricks or rocks

*Perlite and vermiculite can both be found in most garden stores. It is a relatively inert soil additive that looks like small white rocks. This substance soaks up the fuel and releases it slowly, just as it would with water in a garden. Look for products that don't have chemicals, such as plant food, added. If you can't find "plain" vermiculite or perlite, it is okay to use the ones with additives; just don't sit with your face within inches of the flame.

**Be sure the window screen is metal, not plastic. If you don't have any screen scraps sitting in the garage, you can purchase a window screen repair kit, which only costs a few dollars. In such kits are a few patches which will work just fine for this project.

#1 Fill the tin with the vermiculite or perlite to just below the rim. Some people recommend sifting through the perlite and picking out the larger chunks to use in this project. I've never had a problem just pouring it directly from the bag into the tin.

#2 Next, lay out the window screen over the tin and use a marker to trace around the rim of the tin. Cut out the traced shape with your scissors, being sure to round the corners a bit to follow the contour of the tin.

#3 Gently shake the tin back and forth to allow the perlite to settle and level out. Place the cut piece of window screen over the perlite and tuck the edges down into the tin. You might need to trim a little here and there to make it fit nicely.

I've found using a Popsicle stick works great for pushing down the corners.

#4 Carefully pour the alcohol directly onto the screen. You don't need a lot; just 3 tablespoons will suffice in most cases. After closing your fuel bottle and placing it well away from the tin, light a match and place it directly onto the screen.

The alcohol fumes should light instantly. Be advised, alcohol burns very hot and the flame can be difficult to see. If you aren't sure whether the stove lit or not, slowly move your palm near the stove to feel for heat.

#5 When cooking over this stove, you can't place your pan directly on the tin as that will smother the flame. Instead, use small bricks or rocks placed on either side of the tin to support your pan. Three tablespoons of alcohol should be enough to bring a liter of water to a boil without any trouble. If you find you need to add more alcohol, extinguish the flame first! Let the stove cool for a few seconds, then add the alcohol. To do otherwise is to invite disaster.

#6 I prefer to let the stove run out of fuel before storing it, simply because I don't like the idea of my stove possibly leaking drops of fuel into my pack. If you need to extinguish the flame for any reason, though, simply flip the lid closed.

FIRE

The ability to get a fire going in all manner of weather is a crucial survival skill. You can increase your odds of success quite a bit by always having at least a few fire starters and some tinder with you. Commercial fire starters come in a variety of shapes, sizes, and effectiveness. I've used many of them myself and most of them work fairly well. But with just a little bit of work, you can recycle and reuse some of the stuff you have in your home right now and make your own fire starters that work just as well, if not better, than the store-bought varieties.

Fire requires three things: oxygen, fuel, and a spark or flame. If any one of these is lacking, you're not going to be successful. On the surface, oxygen seems like it would be the least likely to pose a problem. I mean, if there's a significant drop in oxygen levels where you are, you likely have bigger issues than getting a fire started. However, suffocating the fire is one of the most common mistakes I see people make. Those new to the art of fire making have a tendency to rush things and add too much fuel too quickly, smothering the fire. A little patience goes a long way.

The time to gather your fire-making supplies is before you strike your first spark. Make three piles for tinder, kindling, and fuel. Tinder is the first level of a fire and consists of dry, fluffy material that will easily catch a spark or flame. Natural sources include cattail fluff, seed pods, and dry grass. Next is kindling. This category is made up of sticks and twigs that are small and thin. Think the size of a pencil or thinner. The drier they are, the better, of course.

Finally, the fuel segment is made up of larger sticks and eventually logs. The fuel should be stacked near your fire, both for convenience and so it can dry out if it happens to be wet. If you build a large stack of firewood, then sit between it and your fire; you'll benefit from the fire's heat reflecting back from the stacked wood.

All of these components should be gathered and piled up near your campfire location before you get started. The last thing you want is to have a newly lit fire starve and go out because you ran out of kindling. Gather and pile up way more kindling and fuel than you think you'll need to get the fire going. For kindling, gather a full armload or two and double that for the fuel.

When gathering kindling and fuel, look for low-hanging, dead branches still attached to trees. They are likely to be much drier than what you'll find on the ground. If everything is damp because of the weather, you can baton branches to get to the dry wood inside (see page 66).

« TEEPEE FIRE »

Perhaps the easiest fire lay for new folks is the teepee. Start by leaning several pieces of kindling together in a teepee shape. Leave one side a bit more open and place your tinder inside. If you're using a fire starter as well, place it into the teepee and cover it a bit with the tinder. Light the fire starter or tinder, and as it burns it will (hopefully) light the kindling. As the kindling begins to burn, carefully lean larger pieces of wood around the kindling, again following the teepee shape. As the wood is consumed, the teepee will eventually collapse down on itself. Continue adding fuel one or two pieces at a time as needed to keep the fire burning.

Fire making requires practice, ideally under a variety of different weather conditions. Learn how to do it well now, before you truly need it to survive the night.

« MELTING WAX »

Several of the projects in this book involve melting wax at some point or another. Rather than repeating the instructions for each of those projects, I've referred you back here as needed.

You don't need to go out and purchase blocks of wax. The best sources for wax to be used in these projects is old candles and/or crayons. Most parents have boxes and boxes of broken crayons. All you need to do is remove the paper wrappers from them. In my experience, though, it is best to stick with brand names, as the wax is of higher quality. As for candles, scented or unscented matters not for our purposes.

If you don't have candles or crayons, pick them up for pennies at thrift stores or rummage sales.

» MATERIALS

Small pot

Soup can (empty, clean)

Wax (crayons, candles, or both)

Oven mitt

Thin stick

#1 Get a pot of water heating on your stove. You'll only need 2 inches of water in the pot. As that heats up, fill about 3 inches of the soup can with broken crayons and candles. The smaller the chunks, the faster it will all melt.

#2 Once the water is just below boiling, put the can in the pot. If need be, add a little more wax to keep the can from floating up. Keep the water at a steady simmer. While you won't "burn" the wax by having the heat too high, a rolling boil will bounce the can around.

#3 As the wax begins to melt, use a thin stick or twig to stir it and break up chunks. While you could use one of your kitchen utensils for this purpose, you'll obviously end up with wax all over it. You may find it necessary to hold the can while you stir.

#4 If needed, you can add more wax chunks as you go along, but I've found it easiest to melt small batches at a time.

#5 You don't have to use the improvised double-boiler approached outlined above, either. That's just the best way I've found to melt wax indoors without damaging any kitchenware. We often have campfires in the backyard and frequently melt wax and make fire starters while we're having s'mores and such. We just place the can of wax on an old grill grate propped up over the campfire.

« THE ORIGINAL DIY »
FIRE STARTER

Okay, I'll confess that this one probably wasn't the very first DIY fire starter ever conceived, but it for darn sure is probably the most common today. The reasons are that it is very easy to assemble and it works very well. Even if you've used them before, read on because you might learn a new trick or two.

❯❯ MATERIALS

Cotton balls
Petroleum jelly
Plastic sandwich bag

#1 Put a handful of cotton balls into a plastic bag and add a dollop of petroleum jelly. Close the bag and mash the cotton and jelly together, really working the jelly into the fibers of the cotton balls.

 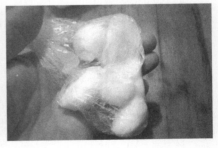

#2 That's it, you're done. I said it was easy, didn't I?

#3 When using one of these fire starters, unroll the cotton a bit, creating more surface area to catch sparks from your chosen fire lighting device. The larger the surface area, the larger the flame, thus a better chance of getting your tinder lit.

#4 For storing these in your pack or kit, I recommend using either an old 35mm film canister or a waterproof match case, such as what I'm using here. The cotton balls can be difficult to scoop out, though. What I do is tie a piece of  string to one cotton ball and jam that one down to the bottom of the container.

#5 Keep the free end of the string outside the container then fill the container with the rest of the cotton balls. Loop the string into the container on to the top cotton ball, then close the container. When you need to pull out a cotton ball, grab the string and gently pull. It will raise the whole stack of cotton balls, allowing you to grab the one you need very easily.

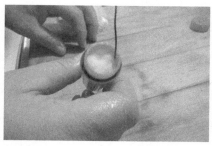
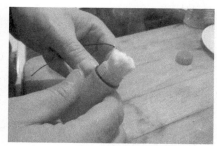

« EGG CARTON FIRE »
STARTERS

This fire starter is familiar to just about any Boy Scout. The reason for that is simple. Egg Carton Fire Starters are incredibly easy to make and to use. Plus, everything you need for them is likely at home already.

» MATERIALS

Cardboard egg carton

Dryer lint or 12 cotton balls

Melted wax (page 54)

Matches, lighter, or spark

#1 Open the empty cardboard egg carton and fill each of the little egg holders with lint or cotton balls.

#2 Then, pour melted wax over each of them, completely covering the lint or cotton balls. Once the wax has cooled and hardened, break the carton up into individual sections.

 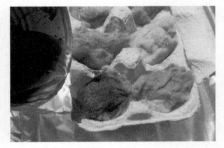

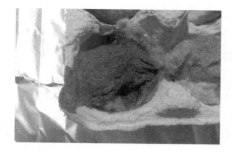

#3 To use, tear open one side of the cardboard section, exposing the fiber inside. Light the cotton or lint with a match, lighter, or spark.

#4 It is important to note that only lint from natural fiber clothing, such as cotton, will work. If you wear a lot of man-made fabrics, you'll need to get lint from another source. A package of cotton balls is incredibly cheap, though.

#5 As you'll find out, these are actually rather heavy, and for that reason I tend to use them just for around the house rather than in my survival kits. They work great for getting a fire going in the fireplace or wood stove.

« SELF-IGNITING FIRE »
STARTER

Like Fire Straws (page 63), this is a waterproof fire starter. Even better, this one incorporates an ignition device, making it sort of a one-stop-shop when it comes to getting a fire going quickly.

» MATERIALS

A few feet of toilet paper

Strike anywhere matches

Melted wax (page 54)

Pliers

Sheet of waxed paper or newspaper

#1 Start by tearing the toilet paper into individual squares, then tearing each of those in half.

#2 Take two of the strike anywhere matches, hold them together, and slip one end of a toilet paper half between them. Wrap the toilet paper around the matches, keeping the top edge just below the heads of the matches.

#3 Using a pair of pliers or a similar tool, dip one end of the wrapped bundle into the melted wax, as far as you can go. Place the bundle on waxed paper or newspaper to cool. Once the waxed bundle has hardened, which only takes 1 to 2 minutes, dip the other end into the melted wax, completely covering the entire bundle, and let it dry.

#4 To use, rub some of the wax off of the match head and strike as you normally would. As the match lights, it will ignite both the toilet paper and the wax, burning for a few minutes with a high, hot flame.

#5 It is vitally important to use strike anywhere matches with this project. Anything else will lead to less than optimum results. Also, avoid using matches that have been previously treated in some way to make them waterproof. Just plain old strike anywhere matches are best for this project.

#6 I have found that sometimes the wax doesn't want to adhere to the match heads. A quick fix is to wrap the toilet paper so it covers the heads before dunking the matches into the wax. When you use the fire starter, just peel that bit away from the heads and you should be good to go.

« COTTON PAD FIRE »
STARTER

Cotton pads are sometimes called makeup removers or something similar. They are basically a flattened-out cotton ball, but with a little more substance. They might be a bit more expensive than cotton balls, but are still incredibly cheap. Because the resulting fire starters are flat, they store very well in an Altoids tin or similar container.

» MATERIALS

Melted wax (page 54)

Cotton pads

Pliers

Sheet of waxed paper or aluminum foil

Your choice of ignition device

#1 Once the wax is melted, use pliers or a similar tool to dip the cotton pads into the wax, covering each pad about halfway or so. Set them on wax paper, aluminum foil or a paper plate to cool, then dip the other side of the pads, covering them completely with wax.

#2 To use, simply crack one in half, exposing the cotton fluff inside. Light the cotton with your choice of ignition device and you're off to the races!

« FIRE STRAWS »

Most of us visit fast food restaurants far more often than we should. Next time you finish gulping down your burger and fries, don't throw away the straw from your soda or shake. While you could just buy a box of plastic straws at the store, I've found that the ones you get at most fast food joints tend to be a bit larger, which makes this project a little easier. Fire straws, when assembled properly, are 100 percent waterproof.

» MATERIALS

Scissors

Plastic drinking straws

Ignition device and candle

Pliers

Dryer lint or cotton balls

Petroleum jelly

Small plastic sandwich bag

Toothpicks

Match, butane lighter, or spark

#1 With a pair of scissors, cut the straws into halves or thirds. The length is a matter of personal preference. I like them short enough to fit into an Altoids tin. Next, light the candle and hold one end of each cut straw 1 to 2 inches from the flame. When the straw begins to soften, crimp it closed with the pliers.

#2 Put the lint or cotton balls into a small plastic sandwich bag and add a dollop of petroleum jelly. Close the bag and mash the jelly and lint together. You want the fibers thoroughly soaked.

#3 Stuff the now-slimy fibers into the open end of the straws, using the toothpicks to pack it in. Leave about ½ inch of space at the open end of each straw.

#4 Once all of the straws are filled, seal them the same way you did at the outset.

#5 To use, slit the side of a fire straw and pull out some of the fibers. Light them with a match, butane lighter, or spark. As the fibers burn, the plastic will ignite as well. While there may be a slight offending smell from the burning plastic, it lasts only a few minutes. Remember, we're talking *survival* here. As long as you don't lean down and directly inhale the fumes, you'll be just fine.

« FIRE FROM ELECTRICITY »

This fire starter has become somewhat well-known, but I'm including it here for those who may not have seen it yet. It is quite cool, actually, and kids in particular seem to get a kick out of it.

While any battery will work, many prefer to use a 9-volt, as it has both positive and negative terminals at the top of the battery, making things easy.

» MATERIALS
Battery
Extra-fine steel wool

#1 For this project, all you do is connect the positive and negative battery terminals with a piece of steel wool. The wool will quickly begin to heat, glow, and flame up.

#2 If you're using a 9-volt battery, just jam the top of the battery into a small pile of steel wool. Otherwise, you'll need to make a thin "string" of steel wool to reach the top and bottom of a standard battery.

#3 In order to use this technique to get a campfire going, you'll first want to sort of bury the steel wool under your other tinder, then "spark" it with the battery. The alternative is to try handling burning steel wool, which isn't going to be a whole lot of fun.

« BATON FIREWOOD »

Batoning firewood is a practice fairly well-known to bushcrafters and others who spend a fair amount of time in the forest. It can be useful when your available firewood is wet, as you'll be splitting the wood, exposing the dry interior. It is also used to process firewood into thinner kindling, whether you need it for getting the fire going or keeping your fire small, such as when using a Brick Rocket Stove (page 41).

It is important to understand that the knife used to baton firewood needs to be robust and of good quality. A cheap knockoff from the dollar store isn't going to cut it, no pun intended. You need a strong blade and the knife should have a full tang. This means that the metal that makes up the blade runs all the way through the handle as one continuous piece. My personal favorite knives include the GNS Scandi by L.T. Wright Knives and the Bushlore by Condor Tool and Knife. In the photos, I'm using a Becker BK9.

The length of the blade will determine the maximum thickness of the firewood you can baton. If your blade is 4 inches long, you'll be able to baton firewood up to about 2.5 inches thick. As for firewood length, I like to stick with pieces about 3 feet long or less. That said, I've successfully batoned lengths of 5 feet or more, more for grins and giggles than anything else.

» MATERIALS

Firewood   Knife

#1 You'll need two pieces of wood, one that you are going to baton and the other to use as your striker or hammer. That one should be about 18 inches long, and it should be strong. Thickness is a matter of preference, but you want it thin enough to hold comfortably.

#2 Start by holding the firewood in one hand and the knife in the other. The bottom of the firewood should be on a firm surface, such as packed earth, a tree stump, or perhaps a flat rock. Wedge the knife blade into the end of the wood, roughly in the middle. You'll need at least 1 to 2 inches of the blade to extend beyond the wood.

#3 Hold the knife handle in one hand and firmly hammer on the knife blade with the other.

#4 Once the blade bites into the wood completely, concentrate your blows on the exposed part of the blade. Slowly, you'll drive the blade all the way through the wood, splitting it in half.

« EXPEDIENT FIREWOOD »
STORAGE

During the aftermath of a disaster, cooking over an open fire might be your best option. If the power is out, microwave ovens and electric stoves aren't going to be operating. Many of us have patio fire pits or similar amenities for our backyard entertaining. These also work great for heating up soup or boiling water. You might find, though, that you'll be using a bit more fuel than usual when the fire isn't just about ambiance. That being the case, you can cobble together this quick and easy firewood storage hack to keep the fuel within easy reach.

» MATERIALS
2 full-size cinder blocks   2 (8-foot) two-by-fours

#1 Place the cinder blocks side by side on a level surface.

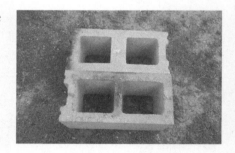

#2 Cut each of the two-by-fours in half, giving you 4 pieces, each about 4 feet long. Place the ends of the boards into the spaces in the cinder blocks, paying particular attention to the placement of the boards relative to the position of the blocks.

#3 If you think of the boards as levers pulling in opposite directions, you want each set of levers to pull against each other in the same cinder block. Otherwise, you could end up with blocks rolling from the pressure.

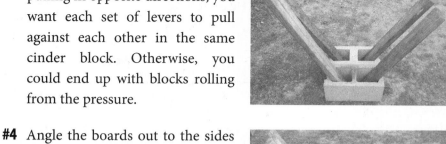

#4 Angle the boards out to the sides and begin stacking the firewood. While this setup isn't really suited for thick, heavy wood, you could put a few larger logs at the bottom without hurting anything. Just avoid making the stack top-heavy.

#5 This is a great solution for temporary stacks of firewood. It keeps the fuel off the ground and easy to grab.

« FIRE KIT »

The fire kit should be a part of your overall survival pack. While I recommend keeping a butane lighter and a bit of tinder in your pocket as well, the fire kit is your primary means of getting a blaze started. It need not be huge nor elaborate. Instead, it is just a collection of the tools you'll need, all kept in one place for easy access.

A fire kit should have multiple ignition devices. Redundancy is the name of the game. Possible ignition devices include:

• Butane lighters
• Strike anywhere matches
• Ferrocerium rod and striker
• Flint and steel

» MATERIALS

In this kit, I have:

Camera case, for storage

Dryer lint in a plastic bag

Char cloth in a small metal tin

Ferrocerium rod and striker

1 WetFire Cube (a commercially produced fire starter)

Magnesium shavings in a plastic bag

Butane lighter

2 tinder tabs

A handful of strike anywhere matches in an old prescription pill bottle

#1 Personally, I tend to favor a ferrocerium (ferro) rod as my primary ignition device and save the others for backup. A ferro rod and a little skill will light hundreds of fires.

#2 For this fire kit, I used an old camera case for the container. I picked up the camera case for about a buck at a local thrift store. Camera cases often make for excellent kit containers because not only are they cheap, they're fairly durable. There is plenty of room in the camera case for me to add other fire starters as well. But, even with just these items, I have three different ignition devices and several different fire starters.

#3 The fire kit should also include a few different ready-to-light fire starters, such as Fire Straws (page 63), Cotton Pad Fire Starters (page 62), or The Original DIY Fire Starters (page 56).

#4 The container you use for your fire kit is a matter of personal choice. The size of the container will be contingent upon the size of your survival pack. In general, something the size of a camera case or smaller should suffice.

#5 One last vital component of your fire kit is an empty zip-top bag. When you're out in the field and are taking a breather from hiking, look around and see if you can locate any natural sources of tinder, such as seed pods or cattail fluff. Collect it and store it in the plastic bag. When it comes to  getting a fire going, use that instead of your DIY items or store-bought fire starters. This is all about conservation of resources. The supplies in your fire kit are obviously finite resources. If that's all you have to use, you'll run out eventually. Therefore, if you're able to use natural resources instead, you'll extend the overall lifespan of your fire kit.

LIGHTING

Man has always been a little fearful of the dark. There's a reason for that, of course. Without light, the boogeyman can more easily sneak up behind us. Don't laugh at that, either. How many times have you, a reasonably intelligent and rational adult, gotten the heebie jeebies walking up the stairs from a dark basement? Yeah, I thought so.

I'll readily admit that I'm something of a flashlight junkie. I'm always on the lookout for something better, something with more lumens but in a smaller size. I have several great portable lights. My current favorite is the Streamlight ProTac 1AAA, which provides a ton of light yet is small enough to slip into a front pants pocket and never get noticed.

In this section, we're going to cover a range of projects that will help to light up the night. Some use fire, others use battery-powered LEDs. All are fairly inexpensive and easy to implement. On top of that, all of them will provide sufficient light to settle your nerves and hopefully keep you from banging your shin on the coffee table.

Admittedly, none of them is going to compare favorably to a flashlight throwing out 750 lumens with the click of a switch. But these projects will allow you to conserve your battery in that flashlight so it still has juice for when you truly need it.

« ALTOIDS TIN CANDLE »

After you've made several fire starters using melted wax, odds are you'll have some wax left over. The Altoids Tin Candle is a great way to use the remaining wax. What some folks do is keep the tin they use for the candle in the same box as their wax-melting gear. They add wax to the tin each time they make fire starters and such, allowing it to build up over time.

» MATERIALS

Altoids tin   Melted wax (page 54)

2 tea lights

#1 Every candle needs a wick. I've found an easy method is to use tea lights. Remove the metal cups from two tea lights. Under the candles you'll see a metal disk, to which is attached the wick. Gently remove the disk and pull the wick through.

#2 Melt your wax and add the two wickless tea lights to the mix so they don't go to waste. When the wax is ready, pour a bit into the bottom of the Altoids tin. Then, before it cools, position the two wicks an even distance apart, using a toothpick if needed to push the metal disks down. It should only take 1 minute or less for the wax to cool enough to keep the wicks in place. Then, pour in the rest of the wax and let it cool.

#3 Why not just toss the two tea lights into the Altoids tin and be done with it? More wax means your homemade candle will last longer. If you wanted, you could add more wicks when you start out, as more wicks will mean more heat given off. Great for chilly nights when the power goes out and takes the heat with it.

« CRAYON CANDLES »

Crayons are wax, just like candles. It stands to reason that they will burn fairly well. While crayon candles will never replace "real" candles, they work well enough for emergency purposes. Like any open flame, you should take precautions to prevent fires.

» MATERIALS

Crayons   Aluminum foil

Sharp knife or razor   Matches or lighter

#1 Break or use the razor to cut the crayon just at or below the line where the paper ends.

#2 The idea here is to use the paper as something akin to a wick. Light the paper and you're basically done with the project. Each crayon will burn anywhere from 8 to 12 minutes or so. Shorter crayons will obviously burn less than longer ones.

#3 The hardest part of this project is figuring out how you will keep the crayon/candle upright and stable. I've seen a few different solutions to this problem, but the easiest is probably to melt some wax onto a square of aluminum foil and stick the crayon to it.

#4 Again, this is nowhere near a perfect solution for emergency lighting. But it'll do in a pinch, buying you some time to come up with a better approach.

« ALTOIDS TIN OIL LAMP »

Should all of your candles come up missing when you're caught in a power outage after sundown, here's a great project that will take just a few minutes and put out a steady light for a long time. The best part is, you most likely have everything you need for this project at home already.

» MATERIALS

Altoids tin

4 inches of cotton rope or similar

Scissors

½ cup cooking oil

Lighter

#1 First, you'll need to determine what you'll be using for the wick. It will need to be made from a natural material, such as cotton. Anything else will just melt. Once you've chosen the wick, you'll know how large the hole in the lid will need to be.

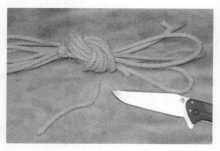

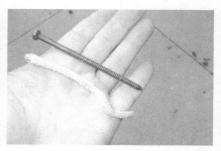

#2 Using a nail or drill, make a hole in the lid, roughly centered, that will be just large enough for the wick to slide through. You're going to want the wick to be snug, so don't make the hole too big. Also, make a small hole in one corner of the lid. This allows air to get into the tin.

#3 Slide the wick through the hole, leaving an inch or less exposed above the lid. The wick should be long enough such that about 3 inches or so of it will coil up into the oil under the lid.

#4 Fill the tin with cooking oil. Olive oil works best, as it is odorless when it burns, but any cooking oil will work. Be careful not to overfill the tin.

#5 Close the lid and let the oil soak into the wick. This might take a few minutes. Use that time to clean up your mess and find your lighter. After lighting the wick, if it seems too smoky, try trimming the wick a bit (after blowing out the flame, of course).

#6 When storing this expedient lamp, be sure to empty the oil from it first. Because of the holes in the lid, it would be far too easy to accidentally spill oil if it is knocked around.

« SOLAR LANDSCAPE » LIGHTS

It seems like almost every home in America has a set of solar lights lining the walk to the front door. They are fairly inexpensive and, for the most part, work pretty well at lighting up the way. It is important to note, though, that their uses aren't limited to the outdoors.

» MATERIALS
Solar landscape lights

#1 After these lights have been in the sunshine all day, you can bring them indoors to provide light through the night. Granted, they aren't very bright, but if you place two or three of them together, they will light up the area enough to prevent you from tripping on an end table. Plus, there might very well be times when you don't want bright lights shining inside your home at night.

#2 When you're shopping for solar landscape lights, concentrate your search on the ones that use AA batteries. You can then let these lights do double duty. Use some of them to provide light in your home at night and others to charge your own rechargeable AA batteries. As with any solar-powered system, it does most of the work for you. Just let it sit in the sun all day long and it will provide you with needed power through the night.

#3 The solar lights should be installed outside in such a way that it is easy to take them down to bring indoors after dark. Some solar landscape lights incorporate some sort of stake that is driven into the ground. Those work well if you put them into large pots of soil on the patio or deck as they'll be easy to pull from the dirt and bring inside. Otherwise, look for solar lights that hang on fence posts, like the one pictured. They easily lift from the post to be brought indoors.

« MILK JUG LANTERN »

Headlamps are possibly even more useful than flashlights. Gone are the days when headlamps were heavy and hot. Today, they use LED bulbs and small batteries. As a result, they are lighter and brighter than ever. However, there are times when you don't really need a bright light shining in front of you, but instead you just need some ambient light in the room. Oil lanterns are great for that purpose, but you can achieve the same effect quickly if you have an old milk jug.

» MATERIALS

LED headlamp   Plastic milk jug

#1 Make sure the milk jug is empty and clean. Fill the jug with water, then wrap the headlamp strap around the jug so the lamp portion faces into the jug. Turn on the headlamp and away you go.

#2 The opaqueness of the jug combined with the water is what allows for such a cool, glowing effect.

SURVIVAL KITS

Fair warning: Building survival kits can be rather addictive. It is quite fun to figure out different ways to provide for your basic needs, all with an eye toward reducing size, weight, and cost of the kit's components.

At the most basic level, a survival kit is a portable assemblage of items that will meet basic needs during a crisis.

In this section, we're going to talk about three basic kits. Keep in mind, though, that your kits don't have to look exactly like the ones illustrated. In fact, if they do, you've made a critical error in judgment. The kits shown in the next several pages were designed specifically for me. They take into account my skill sets, budget, and overall situation. Your kits should be customized for your individual needs and abilities.

There are several categories of needs that any survival kit should satisfy. Depending upon the size of the kit, it might not be possible to cover all of the categories, of course. That's when it is time to prioritize.

Categories of needs:

Water	Medical	Navigation
Food	Fire	Light
Shelter	Hygiene	Signaling

Of these nine categories, the most important ones in the majority of survival scenarios are shelter, fire, and signaling. Hypothermia is a very real danger, even in mild weather conditions. Therefore, it is important to get out of the elements and stay warm. Having something with you for signaling is also desirable. Anything you can do to help rescuers find you will work in your favor.

Naturally, the exact situation at hand will dictate what needs to happen after you've gotten out of the rain or snow. If you're injured, addressing your wounds will take priority over signaling for help. However, if there's a helicopter immediately overhead, getting the pilot's attention would trump putting a bandage on your blistered foot.

A number of great books have been written on the subject of survival kits. Two that I particularly recommend are *Build the Perfect Survival Kit* (2nd Edition) by John D. McCann and *Build the Perfect Bug Out Bag* by Creek Stewart.

« ALTOIDS TIN » SURVIVAL KIT

I have to be honest with you, I'm not a big fan of mini kits. They do serve a purpose, thus the inclusion of one in this book. The problem is, they can offer a false sense of security. The purpose of a mini kit like this one is to allow you to easily carry a small amount of survival gear pretty much anywhere. It isn't a pack you'll have to lug around or a heavy belt pouch. The mini kit fits in your pocket and is often no larger than a thick wallet.

The kit we're illustrating here is one using an Altoids tin as the container. I've seen kits as small as a prescription pill bottle, too. Obviously, you can't carry a ton of stuff in these mini kits, so you need to focus on the absolute bare essentials. Your selection of gear should also take your own skills and circumstances into account. No two kits should ever be absolutely identical.

» IN MY ALTOIDS TIN SURVIVAL KIT, I HAVE:

A small folding knife

LED flashlight

Adhesive bandages

Signal whistle

Pouch of medications (ibuprofen, caffeine, antidiarrheal)

Small brown vial containing water purification tablets

Small butane lighter

Button compass

#1 Not very much at all in the way of supplies, but with this kit I can signal for help, treat water to make it potable, light a fire, take care of stomach upset, and, using the knife, make additional tools or assemble a primitive shelter for the night.

#2 I would never consider this kit to be my primary tool for survival, though. It is kept in my pocket as a backup to a larger kit that I'd hopefully have with me.

« WORKPLACE »
EMERGENCY KIT

Disasters can strike at any time and in any place. The crisis need not be some sort of major, life-changing calamity either. It could be as simple as a bad storm leaving you stranded at work for the night. Here's the thing, folks. Few people would truly relish the idea of spending a single minute more at work than is absolutely necessary. But if it were a choice between spending the night at my desk or in a ditch, I'd be curling up in my office chair.

The Workplace Emergency Kit isn't designed to meet your every need for days on end. It is meant to get you through a night or so, that's it. The kit is small enough to fit under a desk or in a locker without any trouble. It would be best to store the kit at work, rather than just in your trunk. That way, you won't have to worry about forgetting it at home or transporting it back and forth all the time.

With this kit, the focus isn't so much on pure survival as it is on making you comfortable for the evening. After all, odds are you'll have a roof over your head and you won't be worried about people rescuing you. With that in mind, here are my recommendations for the workplace emergency kit.

FLASHLIGHT. If the power were to go out, you'd definitely want a light, if for nothing else than to help you navigate to and from the bathroom. The flashlight doesn't need to be exceptionally expensive, but it should be durable. Face it, you will drop it at least once or twice. You want it to be robust enough that it won't fall apart after it hits the floor accidentally. Streamlight makes a pretty nifty flashlight that charges from a USB port on your computer. You could leave it plugged in to charge every day, then grab it when you need it. Otherwise, keep an extra set of the appropriate batteries for your flashlight in your kit.

FOOD. While cash and coins aren't a bad idea, you can't rely on the vending machines working (again, in case of a power outage) or having a decent selection. It is far better to have a few snacks stashed away in your kit. Stick with things that will last a long time, such as dried fruits and nuts, granola bars, and such. Most of us work in a climate-controlled environment. If there's little worry about things melting or going bad due to heat, feel free to toss in a chocolate bar, too.

WATER. A few bottles of water should be part of your kit. Hopefully, the building's water supply will be just fine and accessible, as always, but plan ahead in case it isn't. I've known a few people who went so far as to toss an entire case of bottled water under their desk. That's not a bad idea at all and costs only a few bucks. This gives you some extra bottles you could offer up to those who didn't think ahead.

EXTRA CLOTHES. Many of us work in an environment that requires business, or at least business casual, attire. That's all well and good but most of us like to change out of that stuff as soon as we get home and put on something more comfortable. If you'll be stuck at the office all night long, you'll appreciate having had the forethought to toss a pair of sneakers, some thick socks, comfortable pants, and a sweatshirt into your kit.

BLANKET. Around the holidays, many stores have incredible sales on fleece blankets. The blankets are about 5 by 6 feet or so in size, very soft, and typically cost about $10. They roll up fairly small and you could easily toss one into your kit. Remember, the idea here is to make your life a little easier, and while a blanket isn't going to guarantee a great night's sleep at the office, it sure couldn't hurt.

HYGIENE SUPPLIES. You likely won't be able to take a shower, of course, but you'll appreciate having a washcloth and some real soap, rather than trying to use paper towels and soap from the sink dispenser. A toothbrush and tube of toothpaste will also be nice.

BOREDOM RELIEVERS. Sure, if the power is still on, you can entertain yourself for hours watching funny cat videos on YouTube. But just in case, toss a paperback novel, a book of crossword puzzles, or some other sorts of distractions into your kit. You might also toss in one of those portable power chargers for your phone or tablet.

#1 The container I'm using for this kit is simply a canvas shopping bag. As noted earlier, this kit is meant to stay at work, not be carried to and fro on a daily basis. A small bag like this will easily fit under a desk or in a locker. You'll also  notice there is plenty of room for additional items, should you want to include more snacks or something.

#2 The Workplace Emergency Kit isn't truly a *survival* kit in the sense that it isn't really there to keep you alive. Rather, it is more like a *sanity* kit in that the purpose is to keep you from losing your mind when you're stuck at work for the night.

« BELT POUCH »
SURVIVAL KIT

The Belt Pouch Survival Kit is, to my way of thinking, the standard survival kit for venturing into the wild. Keep it on your belt any time you hit the trail, removing it only when you're in camp or back at home. More robust than the Altoids Tin Survival Kit (page 85), it is a far more complete kit. Packed properly, it will meet just about all of your basic needs for at least a short period of time.

For my kit, I'm using a Maxpedition H-1 Waistpack. While I like a lot of Maxpedition's stuff, their products tend to be very pricey. The only reason I have this one is that I found a great deal for it online. In the past, I've used pouches found at various discount retailers and even thrift stores. Don't get too caught up in trying to find the perfect pouch. An old fanny pack will work just fine. My local Goodwill has them all the time for just a couple of dollars each. The idea is to have a fairly complete survival kit you can wear on your person for long periods of time with little discomfort.

Let's run down the list of basic needs and go through what we have in this belt pouch kit to meet each of them.

SHELTER. Obviously, you aren't going to fit a tent or even a tarp in a belt pouch. However, an emergency blanket fits the bill nicely. It will keep the rain or snow off, as well as trap and hold your body heat.

WATER. A water bottle isn't going to be part of this kit. Instead, I'm using the Aqua-Pouch sold by SurvivalResources.com. It is a heavy-duty, plastic pouch fitted with grommets and gussets and designed to hold 1 full liter of water. I keep it folded flat, packaged with some water purification tablets, until I need it.

FOOD. In any survival kit, food can be an issue. It takes up space and is often forgotten between trips, meaning it can end up stale or worse by the time you might really need it. Plus, you really don't have any cooking options, as even the smallest stainless steel cup is going to be too big for the belt pouch. What I do is toss in a couple of granola bars and try to remember to take them out at the end of my trip.

FIRE. I like to use an Altoids tin to hold a small fire kit. In it, I have a butane lighter, some strike anywhere matches, and a small ferrocerium rod with striker. Then, I'll toss in a few Fire Straws (page 63) and a couple of Self-Igniting Fire Starters (page 60).

SIGNALING. A signal mirror and whistle fit very easily into the belt pouch kit. This way, we have both visual and auditory signaling available. I've wrapped my signal mirror with several feet of bank line, giving me some emergency cordage if needed.

NAVIGATION. A small button compass should be sufficient in most cases. Some folks upgrade to a more robust compass, which is perfectly fine.

MEDICAL. Another Altoids tin holds a few adhesive bandages, packets of antiseptic ointment, and some medications (ibuprofen, antidiarrheal). You won't be doing open-heart surgery with this kit, but you'll be able to take care of blisters and scrapes, as well as treat a headache or upset stomach.

HYGIENE. A small bottle of hand sanitizer is about all we're going to be able to include, unless you want to toss in a travel-size toothbrush and tube of toothpaste. The hand sanitizer does double duty, too, as the high alcohol content makes it a decent fire starter.

LIGHTING. I will admit to owning more than a few tactical flashlights. They are well-made, tough, and will last a long time. For the belt pouch kit, you have the space to go with something a little more substantial than a little keychain light. What you may want to do, though, is reverse the batteries when storing the flashlight for long periods of time. This will prevent them from draining if the light is accidentally turned on. Many instructors and other experienced folks favor LED headlamps, which are incredibly useful. If they'll fit in your pouch, go with both.

TOOLS. I've also added a multi-tool as well as a small Swiss Army knife to the pouch, giving me tools to use for building a shelter and such.

The Belt Pouch Survival Kit isn't going to meet your needs for weeks and weeks, of course. But this gear, coupled with some basic wilderness survival skills, should keep you alive until you find your way home or are rescued.

MISCELLANEOUS

What follows are the odds and ends of projects that wouldn't fit nicely into any specific category. That's not to say they aren't useful, though. In fact, the Preparedness Flash Drive may turn out to be the single most important project in the entire book. If you lost everything, and I mean *everything*, the information contained on that flash drive would go a long way toward rebuilding your life.

A couple of the projects in this section utilize 5-gallon buckets. Once upon a time, you could find these for free at just about any restaurant or deli. They would have stacks and stacks of them in back, just waiting for someone to give them a home. Nowadays? Not so much. These buckets have become very popular among preppers, survivalists, and even so-called normal people. They aren't impossible to find, you just need to look harder. Just about any business that serves food will have these buckets at some point or another. They are used to ship a wide range of foods, from pickles to frosting. Check with taverns, bakeries, grocery stores, delis, and restaurants. Some places have taken to selling the buckets on a first-come, first-serve basis. I've heard them going for prices as high as $5 per bucket in some places.

Ask around with friends and relatives, as they might know someone who works in a restaurant or deli and could snag an empty bucket or two for you. As you'll see in the projects to come, the lids are important, too.

« GIFT CARD CORDAGE »
STORAGE

Some form of cordage is an essential component of any survival kit. While it is certainly possible to weave cordage from natural materials, such as plant fibers or strands of inner bark, doing so takes considerable time. A far better solution is to pack several feet of cordage in your kit. The problem with doing so, though, is that it often becomes a tangled mess.

Fortunately, there's a pretty easy solution.

» MATERIALS

Scissors   Cordage

Old gift card or credit card

#1 Using the scissors, cut a small notch in one end of the card. Place the notch in the long side, near the end of the card.

#2 Cut another notch on the opposite side and opposite end of the card.

#3 Wedge one end of your cordage into a notch, leaving about 1 inch or so free. Tie a knot to help it stay in place.

#4 Wrap the cordage tightly around the card. Depending upon the thickness of your cordage, you can go up and down the card several times. When the card is full, wedge the cordage into the open notch and cut the cordage 1 inch or so beyond that point. Or you can loop the free end of the cordage through a few of the loops, as shown.

#5 The most common cordage used among preppers is, without a doubt, paracord. It is incredibly strong for its size and can be disassembled into several thinner strands. However, as of late, I've begun to prefer tarred bank line over paracord in most of my kits. It is thinner than paracord, and while it won't support 500-plus pounds, it'll easily handle anything I'll need it to do. Plus, it doesn't stretch like paracord. Because it's thinner, I can pack more of it on a gift card than I can paracord.

#6 If you opt for bank line or another rather thin cordage, you don't need to cut full notches into the card. Instead, just cut small slits.

« BUCKET CLOTHES »
WASHER

With a power outage comes the lack of modern conveniences, like the use of a washing machine. Granted, if the power outage only lasts a day or two, that's probably not the end of the world. But if it were to become a lengthy situation, well, at some point we're all going to run out of clean underwear, right? This is a handy little contraption for washing small amounts of clothes. Washing clothes by hand is a labor-intensive process. If you have children, this is a great chore for them. Save it for the first time they tell you they're bored.

» MATERIALS

5-gallon bucket with lid
Drill with hole saw attachment
  (optional)

Razor knife
Rubber toilet plunger

#1 Start by cutting a hole in the bucket lid using a drill with a hole saw attachment. If you do not have one, use a razor knife. The hole should be in the center, though that doesn't have to be exact down to the millimeter. The hole should be slightly larger in diameter than the thickness of the plunger handle. If the hole is too big, you'll end up splashing water everywhere.

#2 Next, use the razor knife to cut 3 to 4 holes in the rubber part of the plunger. The holes should be about as big around as a quarter and evenly spaced around the plunger. These holes aren't absolutely necessary, though. All they do is allow the plunger to travel through the water a little easier. For reasons that will become obvious, it is best if this plunger is brand new, rather than one you've used after Taco Tuesday.

#3 To use, simply place a few items of clothing into the bucket, pour in enough water to cover the clothes, and add a bit of detergent. Immerse the plunger and feed the handle through the hole in the lid. Close the lid tight. Work the plunger up and down and side to side. This is your agitator. You don't need to go hog wild like you're churning butter, either. A steady rhythm will work better than fast and violent.

#4 Check the clothing after a few minutes. If the items still seem dirty, agitate again for a bit. Obviously, the dirtier the clothing, the longer this will take.

#5 You'll need to rinse the clothing before you hang it to dry. You can either use a separate bucket for this or dump out the sudsy water and replace with clean. Don't just dump the water onto the ground, though. Save it for use in your toilet tank if the water isn't running.

« PORTABLE HEAT »

Where I live in the upper Midwest, it gets dangerously cold in the winter. If the furnace goes out for any reason, indoor temperatures plummet. Space heaters and the like work great, provided that electricity is available. This project allows you to heat a small room without the use of electricity or other utility services.

» MATERIALS

Several rocks

Metal bucket, such as an ash bucket from a fireplace

Metal tongs or shovel

Cinder block or large patio paver

#1 If you have a fireplace or wood stove, you're already ahead of the game. You should be using it to keep at least one room warm. With this project, you can transfer some of that heat to another room. If you don't have a fireplace or wood stove, you can use a patio fire pit or even a campfire. Place a few rocks, each about softball size or so, along the base of the fire. Let them absorb heat for 15 to 20 minutes or so, then carefully transfer them to the metal bucket using the metal tongs or shovel.

#2 Carry the bucket into a small room, such as a bedroom, and place it on a cinder block or patio paver placed on the floor. You don't want to place the bucket directly on the floor, as it will surely damage carpets or other flooring materials.

#3 The rocks will radiate heat for quite some time. The larger the rocks, the more heat they will absorb and then radiate, but the longer they will also take to heat up. You want to be sure you don't overload the bucket, as struggling with a load of hot rocks is not advisable.

#4 It is also important that the rocks you use are not from a wet source, such as a river bed or lake shore. If they have absorbed water, that water could turn to steam and cause the rocks to crack or even explode. What I've done is collect a small pile of rocks from roadsides and such, then placed them outside near my patio. I keep them there as decoration but this also serves to keep them dry.

« BUCKET TOILET »

If a disaster affects the water, you might end up losing indoor plumbing for a bit. In the short-term, you can manually fill the toilet tank and flush as usual. However, if the sewage lines get backed up, that won't be an option. While using a tree out back might be doable for some, if it is the dead of winter, you might not want to risk frostbite in your nether regions.

» MATERIALS

5-gallon bucket with lid

Sand or cat litter

Pool noodle or pipe insulation (optional)

Razor knife

Baking soda or powdered laundry detergent

#1 Place a few inches of sand or cat litter in the bucket. Wrap the foam noodle or insulation around the rim of the bucket (if using) to measure, then cut to a length about 8 inches shorter. Slit the entire length, then slip it over the lip of the bucket. This gives you something of a cushioned seat. They do make toilet seats that are specially fitted for 5-gallon buckets. You can find them at larger camping stores. But this should do in a pinch.

#2 After each use, sprinkle a little sand as well as baking soda or powered laundry detergent over the leavings to help cut down on odor. You will need to empty and refill the bucket regularly. If you have the space available outside, dig a hole a few feet deep and dump the bucket there. Be sure this hole is at least 200 feet from any open water source, such as creeks or lakes.

#3 You could also forgo the initial use of the sand or litter and line the bucket with a heavy-duty garbage bag. This works fairly well, but you'll need to change the bag after a few uses. Otherwise, it can get quite heavy and you risk tearing the bag as you carry it, which would not end well for anyone involved.

« CLOTHESPIN ALARM » TRIGGER

I first came across this basic principle when I was leafing through an old US Army field manual on booby traps. I was all of about 12 at the time and was fascinated by such things. While the original design noted in the field manual was to incorporate this trigger into some sort of explosive device, here we're just using it to raise an alarm.

» MATERIALS

Electrical wire

Battery-activated alarm device

Battery

Wooden clothespin with a spring

Small, thin piece of wood, cardboard, or plastic

Trip wire

#1   The first thing you'll need to do is build a basic circuit running from the alarm you're using and the battery. Run a wire from the positive connection of the alarm to the positive end of the battery. Do the same with the negative connection of the alarm and the negative end of the battery. If you do this correctly, the alarm should sound.

#2   Now that you've confirmed the alarm circuit works, we'll interrupt the circuit with our alarm trigger. Disconnect the wire from the positive terminal on the battery. Remove an inch or so of the insulation from the free end of the  wire, then wrap the wire around one of the jaws of the clothespin.

#3 Next, take a new wire and remove the insulation from the end, then wrap it around the other jaw of the clothespin.

#4 When the clothespin is closed, the two wires need to come into contact with one another. Run this new wire from the clothespin to the positive terminal on the battery. As before, if you've wired everything properly, the alarm should sound.

#5 Open the clothespin and insert a thin piece of wood. Cardboard will work, too, as will plastic or any other nonconductive material. We'll call this piece of material the "interruptor." Attach your trip wire to the interruptor. What I often do is drill or punch a small hole in the interruptor, then use that hole as a place to which I tie my line.

#6 Position the alarm in such a way that the clothespin is attached to something fairly stationary, such as a wall or a heavy piece of furniture. The trip wire runs from the interruptor to another fixed point, like a nail or screw attached

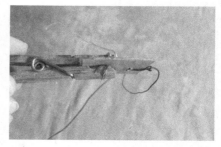

to the wall at the opposite side of the hallway. If both the clothespin and the other end of the trip wire are both firmly anchored, the trip wire will pull the interruptor from the clothespin when the wire is tripped.

#7 Obviously, the wires you use to create the circuit between the alarm, battery, and clothespin can be as long as necessary, provided they are securely attached where needed. This allows you to place the trigger in one place and the actual alarm where you'll hear it.

« BUCKET MOUSETRAP »

Vermin and pests can really do a number on food storage. The moment you become aware that there's something getting at your goodies, you need to take action in order to preserve what's left. Unfortunately, the typical spring-loaded mousetraps you buy at the store will only catch one mouse at a time. Same goes for the glue traps, though sometimes you might get lucky with a two-for-one on those. With this project, not only can you catch several mice at a time, but you also have the option of either terminating them or allowing them to go free somewhere far from your home.

» MATERIALS

5-gallon bucket
Drill
Soup can, any size
Wire hanger
Peanut butter
Small board or branch

#1 Drill two small holes near the rim of the bucket, directly across from one another. The holes only need to be large enough for the wire hanger to fit through.

#2 Remove the top and bottom from the soup can and wash it out. Remove the label as well.

#3 Straighten the wire hanger and cut it to length. It should be long enough to stretch from one side of the bucket to the other, with a couple of inches to spare on each side.

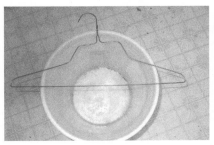 

#4 Run the wire hanger through the two holes, threading it through the soup can. Bend the ends of the wire hanger on the outside of the bucket.

#5 Spread peanut butter on the outside of the soup can. You don't need to use a ton of it, just enough so the mice will be able to smell it and come looking for a snack.

#6 Place the bucket on the floor in the room where you've found evidence of mice. Position a board or branch to act as a ramp for the mice to use to get up to the top of the bucket. The mice will run up the board, walk across the wire hanger, and attempt to get to the peanut butter on the can. The can spins, depositing the mice into the bucket.

#7 If you want to terminate the mice, put several inches of water in the bottom of the bucket. They will not be able to scale the sides of the bucket and will eventually drown. Otherwise, you can leave them in the bucket until you want to relocate them. Put the lid on the bucket, transport the critters to their new home, then dump them out.

« $1 DOOR FORTIFICATION »

Doors are the most common points of entry for home invasions. Makes sense, right? Most people use doors rather than windows, let alone sliding down the chimney or something. As a practical matter, this means fortifying the entry door is important. First, the door should be solidly constructed and ideally have no windows in it. Next, it should have a locking doorknob as well as a deadbolt. When thrown, the bolt should extend at least 1 full inch into the door frame.

Most people, once they get that far, figure that's good enough. In this project, we're going to greatly increase the protection of the entry door, spending all of perhaps $1 on the materials to do so.

» MATERIALS

Screwdriver or drill   Wood screws

#1 Open your front door and locate the hinges. Use your screwdriver or drill to remove one screw from the wall side of one of the hinges. Just one screw from one hinge, that's all. Odds are that screw is fairly short, maybe 1 inch or so in  length. These short screws are great for keeping the door upright and attached to the wall, but afford no real protection. An intruder could just kick the door down along the hinge side. We're going to replace those short screws with longer ones.

#2 Count the total number of screws used to attach the hinges to both door and wall. Typically, that's six screws per hinge. Take the screw you removed down to your local hardware store and find wood screws that are the same diameter (thickness) as the one from your door, but at least 2½ to 3 inches long. Buy enough screws to replace all of the ones on your door.

#3 When you get home, replace each screw one at a time. Doing it this way prevents you from having to take down the door and then rehanging it. On the wall side, the longer screws will go through the door frame and dig into the stud,  affording you much more protection. On the door side, the longer screws will be much stronger as well.

« COUPON STACKING »

Few would argue that coupons can save you money at the grocery store. However, some folks just don't see it as being worth the hassle. Finding a coupon in the paper, cutting it out, carrying it to the store, making sure the item matches the coupon—all in an effort to save a lousy quarter. Heck, you can often save that much just by buying the store brand, right? Here's the thing, though. If you're smart and you're willing to do just a little bit of homework, you can save a considerable amount of money when you're shopping.

» MATERIALS

Coupon inserts from the newspaper   Ads from local stores

#1 There are two basic types of coupons. The ones you find in the coupon inserts from the newspaper are called manufacturer coupons. These can be used at just about any store that sells the products. The second type is store coupons,  which are found either in the store ads or perhaps in the store itself. These coupons can only be used at that store.

#2 *Stacking* refers to using both types of coupons together to get you a better deal. Here's how it works.

In this week's ad, the grocery store has a coupon for granola bars, 2 for $3. Normally, these sell for $2 each. Just last week, you cut out coupons for that same brand of granola bars; each coupon is $0.75 off one box. By stacking your manufacturer coupons on top of the store coupon, you end up paying $0.75 a box.

Normal retail price: $2 each x 2 boxes = $4

Store coupon: $1 off on two boxes

Manufacturer coupons: $0.75 x 2 = $1.50 off

$4 – $1 (store coupon)–$1.50 (manufacturer coupons) = $1.50 for two boxes of granola bars

#3 Many grocery stores today forgo the whole store coupon business and instead ask you to sign up for their loyalty card to get the savings. Some places call this "paperless coupons." I know many preppers dislike such programs, as they feel they could be used to track purchases for nefarious purposes. If you feel that way, consider signing up for the programs but giving false information. Personally, I feel the savings are worth the infinitesimal risk of Piggly Wiggly knowing how often I buy canned chili.

« PREPAREDNESS »
FLASH DRIVE

In the aftermath of a disaster, it can be critically important to be able to access certain documents. While a copy of your insurance policy might not literally save your life, it sure can make your life easier in the long run when you're picking up the pieces left over from a tornado, flood, or other crisis.

The Preparedness Flash Drive is simply an electronic collection of the documents and information you're most likely to need in an emergency.

» MATERIALS

Computer

Scanner

Flash drive

#1 This project is easy enough but can be rather time-consuming. You might find it best to break it up over the course of a weekend or two rather than trying to do it all at once. The basic idea here is to create and save a copy of all of your important documents. You might find it easiest to connect the flash drive first and create several folders within it. The better organized the data, the easier it will be to find if you're under stress.

» Property Ownership

Deeds to all real estate

Mortgage agreement

Lease agreement

» Insurance Policies

Homeowner/renter insurance

Vehicle insurance (car, boat, RV, etc.)

Disability insurance

Life insurance

» Financial Records

List of all bank accounts

Recent bank statement for each account

Copies of all credit/debit cards (both sides)

Copy of most recent tax return

Safe deposit box information

» Medical Records

Insurance cards for each family member

Prescription cards for each family member

List of all of the family's medical providers

List of all prescribed medications, allergies

Immunization records for all family members

List of blood types for all family members

» Vehicles

List of all vehicles owned

Vehicle ownership records

Loan documents or lease agreement

» Pets

List of all pets

Full medical record for each pet

Photo of each pet WITH family members

» Miscellaneous

Recent photos of all family members

Copy of will

Copy of power of attorney

Copies of birth certificates

Copy of marriage certificate

Copies of all driver's licenses or other identification

Copies of business cards for attorney, accountant, and other professionals

List of important phone numbers for extended family members and other loved ones

Copy of military service records, including discharge paperwork

#2 Some of these records likely have been provided to you, or can be sent to you by the record holder, in electronic format. Just save a copy of those to the flash drive in the appropriate folder. For paper copies, you'll have to scan them in order to make an electronic copy. When doing so, I advise you to make sure to use PDF as the file format. PDF is universally used and can be accessed using any computer. That said, do yourself a favor and download a copy of the Adobe Acrobat Reader program to save on your flash drive, just in case the computer you end up using to access your data for some reason doesn't have the program installed.

#3 Another idea to include in this project will, for most people, be quite labor-intensive, but still worth considering. You might want to include scanned copies of any particularly treasured family photos on the flash drive. Yes, it will take quite some time to go through all of those photo albums as well as boxes of loose photos. But in the event of a house fire or other disaster, at least you'll have the scanned photos. Many of us have multiple SD cards and other media that is storing our digital images. It would be a simple process to highlight, click copy, then paste them into a folder on the flash drive.

#4 Naturally, many of these records are rather sensitive and you won't want people to be able to access them if the flash drive is lost or stolen. Fortunately, you have a couple of options. First, you can password protect the flash drive. This is easily done with any number of free programs available online. Rohos Mini Drive and Comodo Disk Encryption are two options I'm told work extremely well.

#5 The other option is more expensive but is about as secure as you can get. There is a product out there called IronKey. Without getting into all the technical mumbo jumbo, suffice it to say that the IronKey flash drive is not only protected against all hacking attempts, but is physically hardened as well. If an attempt is made to break into the IronKey physically, it will initiate a self-destruct sequence to ensure your data doesn't fall into the wrong hands. As I mentioned, though, it is expensive, with the basic model coming in around $200 or so.

« IMPROVISED GEAR »

While an argument could be made that the vast majority of projects in this book fall under the category of "improvised gear," here we're going to talk about just a few things that really aren't so much projects as they are quick-and-dirty solutions to survival needs.

KNIFE SHEATH. A knife is an extremely valuable and useful tool in most survival situations. Good-quality knives can be rather expensive. A decent compromise is to use a kitchen knife and improvise a sheath for it. Here, I've assembled a quick but sturdy sheath using thin cardboard and duct tape. It isn't a perfect solution, of course, but it'll certainly do in a pinch. You could also use a piece of broken glass with a duct tape handle, or even the blade removed from a small appliance and affixed to a wood or plastic handle. Use your imagination and get creative.

 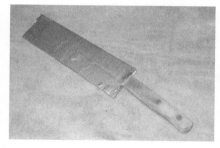

CORDAGE. Before tossing old, irreparable shoes into the trash, be sure to remove the laces. Cordage is always of use in survival situations, such as for shelter building. While it is certainly possible to weave cord from plant fibers and such, doing so is time-consuming.

WIRE TIES. Along the same lines, many parents are familiar with the plastic-coated wire ties that come as part of the packaging in many toys today. They come in other products, too, but toy companies apparently found an incredible deal on these things, as you'll find roughly a bazillion of them inside the box of any average toy. While a pain in the butt to remove, they can be very useful. They are very strong and can be used in many applications where you might otherwise use a nylon zip tie or some type of cordage. Look at it this way—so you've already paid for those wire ties, so you might as well find a use for them.

COTTON SQUARES. Old T-shirts can be used as rags, of course, as just about any homeowner knows. However, another use for them is to cut them into squares to use as toilet paper should your supply run out. Not the most appealing solution for most of us, given how accustomed we are to flushing all evidence of our potty usage, but cotton squares sure beat using leaves from the backyard. Should it come time to put these to use, fill a small bucket with a mild bleach solution and toss the used squares into it. Yeah, you might want a cover for the bucket. When the bucket is full or the supply of squares is running low, wash them with hot water and bleach and be sure to rinse them well.

WEAPON. Old socks could serve a similar purpose as the cut T-shirts above. They could also make for a decent, expedient weapon for self-defense. Toss in a rock about the size of a golf ball, or perhaps one or two dead C batteries, and you've made a sap, or slapjack. Grasp at the open end of the sock and swing the sock at your target. Of course, if there are holes in the toe end of the sock, you'll want to darn it first.

TOOL KIT. Can't afford a good multi-tool? How about a simple pair of pliers? Think about it, most multi-tools consist of a pair of pliers with a knife blade and a few other tools attached in some way. While the whole point of a multi-tool is to have all of these tools in one handy package, that doesn't mean you can't go the old-fashioned route. A small pair of pliers, a folding knife, and a pair of wire cutters and you'll be in business. Nite Ize makes a really great belt pouch system for carrying such tools, and it isn't all that costly, either.

We often get hung up on how certain types of gear are supposed to look. We should be far more concerned about function over form. If it works, keep it. If it doesn't work, move on to the next alternative and test it out. Step outside the box and you'll find a world of possibilities at your fingertips.

« PREPPER USES FOR »
ALUMINUM FOIL

Aluminum foil is incredibly useful to the prepper. It is also very cheap, which makes it even more appealing. Shop around, though, and always go for the heavy-duty foil rather than choosing strictly based on price. The thicker and more durable the foil, the better off you'll be when using it for things other than just covering your casserole.

SCARING BIRDS. If you have fruit trees or shrubs, hang a few strips of foil in the branches. Doing so will help scare off birds that might otherwise be a nuisance to you.

PROTECT TREES IN WINTER. When their normal food sources aren't available due to snow cover and such, some animals will take to eating the inner bark of trees. Protect yours by wrapping the trunk with a few layers of foil. No need to do the entire tree, of course; just the first few feet should be sufficient.

SHARPEN SCISSORS. Fold a small sheet of foil a few times, then cut through it four to five times with the scissors. This is a great way to keep scissors sharp without resorting to a strop block or other device.

POT SCRUBBER. If you're away from home and need to scrub out your cooking pot, crumple up a small piece of foil to use as your scouring pad.

FRYING PAN. While not nearly as good as an actual frying pan, the forked end of a stick may be wrapped a few times with foil to make a makeshift pan. I wouldn't use it for heavy items, but it'll do in a pinch for most things.

BOOT PRINT. Before heading out on a hiking or camping trip, take a moment to make a boot print using a piece of foil. Tear off a section of foil large enough so your foot will fit on it. Take the foil to a grassy area and step on it, slowly but firmly. The boot impression will be very useful to trackers if you end up lost. Put the print on the floor of your front seat along with a note with your name, the date and time you're hitting the trail, and when you expect to return.

RESIZING BATTERIES. If you have a device that uses AA batteries and all you have are AAA, no need to fear. Crumple small balls of foil to place at the ends of the batteries so they make contact with the terminals in the battery compartment.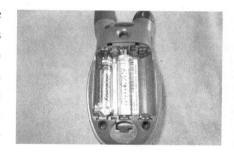

FOOD PACKETS FOR COOKING. Many campers know this trick already. Aluminum foil can be used to make great little single-serve packets to cook right on the coals of a fire. I've heard these called "Hobo Tin Foil Dinners," which is as good of a name as any, I guess. The classic version uses ½ pound of hamburger (the leaner, the better), cut-up potatoes, carrots, and onions, and a bit of butter and seasoning. Lay out a square of foil about twice as big as your food. Plop the food down in the middle and bring up two sides of the foil, folding them together and rolling it down. Then, roll up the ends, making a tight packet. Toss this on glowing coals for about 20 minutes. There are a ton of recipes out there for "foil packet cooking," but feel free to improvise as you'd like.

FISHING LURE. A small piece of foil secured to a hook makes for a dandy little improvised fishing lure. Great for those times when you can't find any natural bait.

« PREPPER USES FOR »
TRASH BAGS

Whether they're referred to as trash bags, garbage bags, or bin liners, they have a ton of uses in addition to just containing your rubbish. When buying trash bags for the following purposes, always look for the heavy-duty variety, sometimes called "contractor grade" bags. These are going to be both larger and more robust than the bags you likely use in your kitchen and bathroom garbage cans. Because of this, they are also going to be a little more expensive. But you don't necessarily need to buy a ton of them, either. One or two boxes will likely suffice for even a moderately lengthy crisis. You'll want a few trash bags in your primary survival kit as well as at home.

TOILET LINER. If the sewage lines are blocked or you just plain don't have water for flushing, empty the toilet bowl as completely as possible, then line it with a trash bag. Replace the bag after just a few "deposits," as you don't want to risk the bag becoming too heavy to lift.

RAINWATER COLLECTION. If you have a bucket or barrel that might be questionable in terms of suitability for collecting rainwater, line it with a trash bag first. Do the same with a hole dug in the ground, a route that will gain you far more water than the vaunted Solar Still (page 9). You'll still want to run the water through a good filter or boil it before consumption.

RAIN PONCHO. If you've ever been caught in rainstorm at an outdoor event like a county or state fair, you've no doubt seen many people scrounging for empty trash bags. Tear a hole for your head and one for each arm and you're in business.

SHELTER ROOF. When building an expedient shelter, a trash bag works rather well as a waterproof, or at least water-resistant, roof. What many do is use brush or sticks as a supporting structure, lay down the bag, then weigh it down with more brush. Sort of a trash bag sandwich.

GROUND COVER. Sitting on the trash bag instead of the damp ground will keep you from getting a wet butt. At the end of the day, you could fill the bag with leaves and pine boughs for a passable mattress. It might not be as comfortable as your bed at home, but the insulation will help you stay warmer through the night.

PACK LINER. Many a hiker or camper has found the usefulness of lining their pack with a trash bag before putting in all of their gear. Most packs aren't waterproof, so adding this layer of protection helps to keep your stuff dry, even in a pounding rain.

WATERPROOFING A BANDAGE. Keeping a wound covered and dry will help prevent infection. If you're facing particularly damp conditions, you can cut or tear a section of the trash bag and bind it over the bandaged wound to keep it dry.

WINDOW COVERING. You may have very good reason to cover your windows at home such that light from your candles or lanterns cannot be seen outside. Use duct tape to secure the trash bag to the inside window frame. Be sure to check your work by going outside at night to see if any light escapes.

FOOD COLLECTION. When foraging for wild edibles, you'll obviously need some sort of container. At home, you probably have plastic bags galore. Out in the wild, maybe not so much.

FINAL THOUGHTS

One thing I'm really hoping is that after reading through this book and trying some of the projects, you come up with a few of your own ideas. Fair warning, though: Not only can this stuff be fun, it can be downright addicting. In fact, you run the risk of becoming so enamored with repurposing and recycling that family members may think you've become a hoarder. That, my friend, is on you, not me. Don't blame me if you find yourself loathe to throw anything away because you think you might have a use for it later. Remember, everything in moderation. Sure, the wire ties found in most toy packaging can be incredibly useful, but you probably don't need 35 shoeboxes full of them.

Then again, who knows what the future might bring. Could be those 35 boxes of wire ties will be all that stands between you and utter anarchy.

Nah, that's just silly. Wire ties can't prevent chaos from ruling the streets. Now, duct tape on the other hand....

INDEX

ACKNOWLEDGMENTS

This one took a lot of work, much more than I recall from my previous books. As always, I must first thank my beautiful, patient, and extremely supportive wife, Tammy. Darlin', there's no way I could do all of this without your help.

To my boys, thank you for your help as well. Whether it was taking a few photos for me or just staying out of my hair when I needed to work, I really appreciate it.

To my amigo Chris Golden, having you in my corner means the world to me. Thanks for always watching out for me and keeping me from doing something I'd later regret.

To Bob and Joanne Hrodey, thank you for being so incredibly supportive.

To John McCann, you were a mentor of mine before you even knew I existed. Boy, that sounds kind of creepy, doesn't it? Thanks for watching my back, supporting me, and being a good friend.

To my brothers and sisters in the Bushcraft/Hike/Outdoor trading group, you folks have integrity and loyalty beyond measure. I'm both honored and humbled to be part of the group. Thank you for everything. Special shout outs to Chris Gustafson, Blake Watson, Brad Johnson, Jeff Russell, Hawk Costlow, Eric Messner, David Sabet, and Jeff Turner. You guys all do a great job keeping the group focused and on track. Keep up the good work!

Finally, to my readers. I cannot possibly thank you enough for allowing me to spend some time in your heads. It is because of you that I get to do fun stuff like write books for a living. I promise I will do everything I can to help you along your preparedness journey.

ABOUT THE AUTHOR

Jim Cobb is the author of several books focused on disaster readiness, such as *Prepper's Long-Term Survival Guide*, *Countdown to Preparedness*, *Prepper's Financial Guide*, and the #1 Amazon bestselling *Prepper's Home Defense*. He has been a student of survivalism and prepping for about thirty years. He is the owner of SurvivalWeekly.com, a rather popular disaster readiness resource.

Jim and his family reside in the upper Midwest and he is currently working on several more books.